PRAISE FOR

THE *Unburdened* HEART

Susie plays all the right notes when it comes to addressing the tender and varied subject of hurting. Forgoing cloying and trite, her writing brings a much-needed and appreciated directness to those are broken and presents advice and hopeful perspectives for healing and change.

Julie Barnhill
Speaker and Author of *Scandalous Grace*

Between the covers of *The Unburdened Heart* lies freedom for every heart held captive by unforgiveness. Chapter by chapter, Suzie shares powerful truths and practical teachings that will equip you with courage and strength to not only forgive but also move on and live victoriously in that forgiveness. This is the best book I have read on forgiveness.

Wendy Blight
Author of *Hidden Joy in a Dark Corner*, Teacher and
Proverbs 31 Ministries Speaker

Suzie speaks with the warmth of a friend and the wisdom of a sage to one of our common struggles—forgiveness. Offering down-to-earth help built on a deep scriptural foundation, she reveals a many-layered truth that forgiveness isn't the one-size-fits all proposition we've so often accepted. I feel relief and joy in realizing that God fully acknowledges the difficulties of forgiveness while still holding it up as the healing tonic against bitterness and debilitating anger.

Amy Carroll
Proverbs 31 Ministries Speaker

Suzie fills up our toolboxes not just for today but also for the future. Conflict, hurt and pain are just a part of this world. The Unburdened Heart gives exactly what we need to walk in the freedom Christ died to give us . . . no matter what our circumstances!

Lynn Cowell
Founder of Wise Women . . . Wiser Daughter and Proverbs 31 Ministries Speaker
Author of *His Revolutionary Love* and *Devotions for a Revolutionary Year*

Forgiveness can be fuzzy, and it's easy to get stuck on the journey. But with this book, Suzie builds a safe place to struggle with the questions and walks us through the freedom that forgiving promises.

Carol Davis
Radio Host, 106.9 The LightFM

The Unburdened Heart provides both healing and hope for those who have been affected by circumstances that have left them scarred and scared. While Satan may seek to tightly wind the chains of bitterness, anger and unforgiveness around our wounded hearts by tempting us with wrong thinking and the destructive counter-productive actions that result, this book teaches how to release the hurt and move forward—free, whole and holy.

Karen Ehman
Proverbs 31 Ministries Director of Speakers and Author *LET. IT. GO.*

Virtually all Christians know they should forgive, but few really understand *how*. In this insightful book, Suzie Eller uncovers the blanket of mystery surrounding the hows and whys of forgiveness. She provides a biblical and practical path that leads to the freedom those held captive by unforgiveness so desperately crave. This is a book for all of us.

Donna Jones
Speaker and Author of *SEEK: A Woman's Guide to Meeting God*

More times than not, forgiveness is a process instead of an event. It's costly and painful, yet freeing and beautiful. In *The Unburdened Heart,* Suzie Eller handles this topic with truth and grace. If you've got an unhealed area in your soul, I ask you to go on this journey with her. Trust her to hold your hand and lead you to places of grace and healing. Freedom waits for you on the other side.

Susie Larson
Co-host of Focus on the Family's *Everyday Relationships* with Dr. Greg Smalley
Host of *Live the Promise* and Author of *Your Beautiful Purpose*

Without God's forgiveness, we would all be lost. So why is it so hard to give to others? How do we do lay down the burden of unforgiveness and the resentment and bitterness that accompanies it? With insightful biblical analogies and a warm, inviting tone, Suzie illustrates the effects of unforgiveness and walks readers through theprocess of offering grace and embracing wholeness. This book opened my eyes to the picture of what forgiving like Jesus really means.

Melinda Means
Founder, Mothering from Scratch

I began reading *The Unburdened Heart* with the mindset that my heart was fine, but as I spent time deeply pondering the personal reflection questions Suzie poses, I realized that I had been inadvertently allowing unforgiveness to burden my heart. Suzie's book helped me to let go of hurt and bitterness and experience a spiritual and emotional freedom that I didn't even know I was missing.

Tracie Miles
Author and Proverbs 31 Ministries Speaker

There is incredible freedom in living a life of grace and mercy. Suzie Eller believes that, lives that and shows us how to walk the road to experience that ourselves. Do you need to unburden your heart and experience freedom from the hurts of the past? You can start today by opening the pages of this powerful book.

Jill Savage
CEO of Hearts at Home and Author of *No More Perfect Moms*

Whether you are weighed down with a deep betrayal or yearn to be free of any petty grudges you might be carrying, Suzie Eller provides the tools needed to forgive and grow emotionally and spiritually. She powerfully sharers practical insights and biblical wisdom and challenges and guides us to move beyond our hurts and bitter disappointments into the freedom of forgiveness that God provides.

Georgia Shaffer
Author, Licensed Psychologist in Pennsylvania
Professional Speaker and Christian Life Coach

Most of us know forgiveness is hard, but Suzie admits it wholeheartedly and then *proves* it by sharing the nearly impossible forgiveness stories of people who have suffered horrific offenses. We witness their unique journeys toward forgiveness—raw, real and gutty—and see that forgiveness can heal the forgiver more than the forgiven. Suzie will take your hand and guide you through the life-changing process of forgiveness. This is one of those books that has the potential to change your life.

Jenny Dean Schmidt
President and Host of *The Channelmom Show*

If you've been carrying a heavy load of hurt, resentment, bitterness or pain, God wants you to be set free. Suzie's book not only shows why we should forgive but also teaches us how to walk through the process.

Leslie Vernick
Licensed Counselor, Coach, Speaker and Author of the Bestsellers *The Emotionally Destructive Relationship* and *How to Act Right When Your Spouse Acts Wrong*

In *The Unburdened Heart,* Suzie Eller invites us on a gentle journey of forgiveness, freedom and peace. With real-life stories threaded throughout and reflective questions she calls "Just You and God" at the end of each chapter, she sheds some much-needed light on why forgiveness is often illusive, complex and definitely easier said than done. This is a great resource for individual or group study, and as you take this journey, you will find hope and healing along the way. I highly recommend it!

Stephanie Shott
Author, Speaker and Founder of the M.O.M. Initiative

I don't struggle with forgiveness . . . or at least I didn't think I did. Suzie's book opened my eyes to the truth. She was thorough in unpacking this struggle, offering biblical examples and practical applications along the way. She addresses all sides of forgiveness—what it is, what it is not, and how God views it—dispels myths surrounding it and shows how to live free from it. Thank you, Suzie, for opening my eyes and lighting a path to freedom!

Carey Scott Wiggins
Speaker and Author of *Let's Get Real: Raising Godly Kids*

FINDING THE FREEDOM
OF FORGIVENESS

THE
Unburdened
HEART

SUZANNE ELLER
Speaker Proverbs 31 Ministries

Regal

For more information and
special offers from Regal Books, email us at
subscribe@regalbooks.com

Published by Regal
From Gospel Light
Ventura, California, U.S.A.
www.regalbooks.com
Printed in the U.S.A.

For privacy, some of the names of the people profiled have been changed. Permission has been granted for personal stories used throughout.

Library of Congress Cataloging-in-Publication Data
Eller, T. Suzanne.
The unburdened heart : finding the freedom of forgiveness / T. Suzanne Eller.
p. cm.
Includes bibliographical references and index.
ISBN 978-0-8307-6512-6 (trade paper : alk. paper)
1. Forgiveness. I. Title.
BJ1476.E44 2013
234'.5—dc23
2012042128

Rights for publishing this book outside the U.S.A. or in non-English languages are administered by Gospel Light Worldwide, an international not-for-profit ministry. For additional information, please visit www.glww.org, email info@glww.org, or write to Gospel Light Worldwide, 1957 Eastman Avenue, Ventura, CA 93003, U.S.A.

To order copies of this book and other Regal products in bulk quantities, please contact us at 1-800-446-7735.

Dedication

My husband, Richard, knows my heart for ministry. He's there when I run straight into the wall of real life, while I'm writing or speaking, with a word of encouragement. I am grateful for a husband who I love like crazy.

I also want to thank Rachelle Gardner, my Books and Such agent who believed in this book from the beginning. I loved your reaction the first time you read it! Thank your for your perseverance in finding it a home.

Thank you to Kim Bangs at Regal. You were a kindred spirit from day one. I love working with you and your team.

A special thank-you to a courageous group of women: Vickie, Megan, Chellie, Janie and Jessica. You are beautiful women, in all stages of forgiving, and you held me accountable as you shared your honest thoughts, your breakthroughs and the emotional mountains you encountered chapter by chapter. There were times that I wept as I read your emails, especially in the "aha" moments. You invited me inside your personal stories, victories and struggles. What a brave group of women! I am indebted to each of you.

Last, I want to thank Leslie, Stephen, Melissa, Josh, Ryan and Kristin, and my grandbabies Elle, Luke, Jane and Audrey. When I define my greatest treasure in one word it is "family." Thank you for being mine.

Contents

Contents

Foreword

I don't know exactly when it started. I just remember feeling angry and frustrated with my husband—almost every single day—on and off for months. One evening after an argument, J. J. told me that no matter what he did or how hard he tried, it was never enough.

He was right, but I didn't know what was wrong with me. I was tired of being mean and miserable, so I started asking God to show me what was going on—to help me figure out how, after seven years of a fairly happy marriage, we had gotten to this ugly place.

Over time, I sensed God was showing me that I wanted J. J. to make up for what my dad had never been as a father to me and as a husband to my mom. I think I was trying to create my own version of "happily-ever-after," and in doing so, I became very controlling and critical.

You see, years as a child in a broken home with a broken heart had led to a significant sense of loss and deep disappointment. But I had never processed, grieved or let go of what I thought I deserved yet didn't have.

My unforgiving heart and unfulfilled hopes had created bitter expectations. I thought if I could get J. J. to be the husband and dad I wanted him to be, maybe my broken past and shattered dreams could be put back together.

I knew I needed to deal with my pain, but I couldn't just forgive and forget it. It wasn't that easy. There were layers of pain, and issues I'd never dealt with. But I took the first step by acknowledging my hurt and giving myself permission to feel it. Then I carved out time each week to unpack the memories and events that led me to this hard place and then allowed God to heal them.

I asked Jesus to help me grieve the loss of things I wanted that I would never have from my dad. And I asked Him to walk me through the steps of forgiving my father so that I could release the anger, abandonment and hurt that had held me prisoner for so long.

It was a process that took time, prayer and courage, but it was worth it. I was worth it. My marriage was worth it.

Suzanne Eller

Like most people, I didn't want to face my pain. I didn't have time and I didn't want to dig it all up. But I am so glad I did! Through it all, God showed me how to let go of my past hurts so I could take hold of hope and the healing that I never thought I would find.

As I worked through what happened in my childhood and how it was affecting my marriage, I realized I needed the help of a friend. I needed someone who had walked a similar road to come alongside me to offer wisdom and another perspective in my healing journey. In the pages of *The Unburdened Heart*, Suzie Eller is that friend. Offering wisdom and a heart full of compassion, Suzie will come along beside you and mentor you each step of the way. Yet, Suzie doesn't just share from a place of knowing about forgiveness; she writes from a place of living it and giving it, when it's hard.

One thing I love about Suzie, and the message she lives, is that she's not a cookie-cutter Christian. She won't just say, "You need to forgive." She knows it's not that easy, but she also cares too much to leave you in that hard place. Instead, she'll take your hand and walk you through the process, sharing her story as you look at yours.

In bringing depth to the layers of a forgiving-life, Suzie will help you explore the different meanings of forgiveness as she walks with you through your unique journey. She'll also introduce you to amazing women and men who have offered their hearts, their stories and their courage to help you recover yours!

Chapter by chapter, Suzie will invite you, even urge you at times, into a place of hope and healing because she wants you to experience the sacred transformation that forgiveness brings.

I hope you'll accept her invitation. It will require time, courage and perseverance; but you are worth what it takes. You see, forgiveness is a gift we give ourselves when we offer it to others. In doing so, we don't forgive so we can forget. We forgive, as we have been forgiven, so that we can be set free from our past and live with confident hope in our future.

Renee Swope
Award-winning Author of *A Confident Heart*
Proverbs 31 Ministries Radio Co-host and Speaker

Introduction

Jesus says to forgive.

Have you ever heard those words? Scripture instructs us about forgiving others, over and over again; and forgiving *is* foundational in living free from bitterness, deep-rooted anger or hurt. But living a forgiving lifestyle is an uneven journey at best. We accept God's grace and then stumble over giving it.

Can I be honest? Forgiveness is hard. It's also complex. Forgiveness requires different levels of effort—from forgiving the neighbor who said those not-so-nice things about your family to forgiving a spouse who cheated, an abusive parent or someone who intentionally harmed you or a loved one.

This is where Christ comes in. Throughout the Bible we see Jesus meeting people right where they are. He met Nicodemus under the stars, in the middle of the night. The conversation began at a point where Nicodemus could ask his scholarly questions and find truth. Later, we see Jesus kneel in the street beside a broken woman crouched in the dust. Even as her accusers aimed stones in her direction, He quietly showed her a new way to live. He began that conversation at the critical point of her greatest need.

As you and I study this topic of forgiveness together, you'll discover that same approach. Rather than toss out a blanket statement of "just forgive," you'll discover how forgiveness can grace you right where you are and unburden your heart so that you can heal and live free.

The word "forgive" has many meanings in Scripture, and it also offers diverse benefits for those who are willing to live as a forgiver. Each meaning offers us significance. One may show us how to forgive injustice or move past the marks of neglect or abuse. And yes, there's even a definition that shows us how to forgive that not-so-nice neighbor.

But it doesn't stop there, because forgiveness offers dignity when it has been stripped away. It allows you to climb up and out of the past and live fully today. It shows you how to accept who and what you cannot change, all the while allowing God to transform you.

Are you surprised that there is not a one-size-fits-all definition of forgiveness? I was too. What remains consistent, however, is that forgiveness is key to God-sized healing. That's why it comes up in Scripture over and over again. Forgiveness matters to God, because you matter to God.

How do I know that?

I've been there. I was once a broken girl raised in a fractured family. One parent struggled with suicidal thoughts that often escalated into scary rages or sank into depression, sweeping me and my siblings, into the current. But it also swept her into that same tide while her husband hid behind a newspaper or spent long hours at a job, oblivious to the cries of help from his hurting wife and children.

One of my earliest memories is of lying in a hospital bed after an emergency appendectomy surgery. It was late at night. I was alone and frightened. I wrapped my tiny arms around my five-year-old body and started singing to soothe myself. I learned early that if anyone was going to take care of me, it was me. This is only one of many unhealthy beliefs I embraced early on.

Later, I became a believer, and God began to alter my way of thinking. For the first time, I realized I didn't have to be tough or put a wall around my heart. But I still struggled. It was hard to trust. It seemed impossible to let down my guard and be myself. I was self-sufficient to a fault, pushing away those who could have shown me an easier path. And I was angry. Deep-down angry. It showed up in surprising ways. Most people didn't realize how hard I worked to keep it at bay.

I began to ask God to help me. As I prayed and read my Bible, I kept running into the word "forgive." I knew this was something God was asking—commanding—me to do. But I ran into mountain-sized questions like:

What about the feelings that won't go away?

What if the person who hurt me is still in denial or destructive?

If I forgive, does it say that his or her behavior was acceptable?

I see joy in the life of others. Will I ever find it?

Over time, I found my answers, and forgiving was not only key but was essential to moving beyond my feelings into a life that God had for me—regardless of my past or whether anyone else changed.

I intentionally pursued forgiveness. I began the process of letting go. Seeing my parent from a viewpoint of compassion changed me, and years later it changed both of us. Let me make you a promise: There *is* incredible freedom in living a life of grace and mercy. But it's not something you just find along the way. Forgiveness is a choice, and it's a journey.

Forgiveness is often tricky and messy because it involves people. It may require digging deep into issues you would rather leave buried. You may hesitate over forgiving when it seems like you are the only one who desires change.

Can I tell you something? You are not alone in this process. Christ comes to you right where you are, even if you are at the place where forgiving someone seems impossible; or when you are willing but unsure of where to begin; or when you've tried over and over again, only to pick those feelings back up, and you are sick of them.

In this book you will meet real people who understand what you are feeling; and yet, most have forgiven under extraordinary circumstances. Each of them started at a point where forgiving someone seemed overwhelming, if not impossible. They desired to climb out and from under the heavy burden that unforgiveness placed on their thoughts, their relationships and on the way they interacted with people and even with God.

Like you, they may have had no idea of what God could or would do as they took that first step; they simply started the journey.

As I wrote this book a few women, in all stages of forgiving, came alongside. They read chapter by chapter and courageously asked questions and shared their honest thoughts. Some of those questions deepened my study, and you'll find some of the questions later in the book.

As you go through this study, keep in mind that you and I will never be perfect (is there such a thing?). But self-discovery, especially when performed under the gentle prodding of the Holy

Spirit, is a courageous act. The journey to an unburdened heart involves risk. Each new step presents the possibility of learning a truth about yourself that may feel uncomfortable; but it also presents the possibility of growth and real change.

Only God encompasses all the many meanings of the word "forgiveness." Yet, there are riches to be found within the pursuit. My prayer is that as time passes, this study will become less about the theory and more about an intimate, personal discovery with your heavenly Father.

PART 1

What is Forgiveness?

1

What Does it Mean to Forgive?

Forgiving is more like writing a book than writing a letter.
When I write a letter, I put my thoughts on paper, sign it,
seal the envelope, and send it. Writing a book involves what seems
an endless cycle of writing and rewriting.

Gary D. Preston, *Character Forged from Conflict*

"Do you want to live free?" I asked the crowd.

Though it was a rhetorical question, one woman stood. She waved her hand in the air. "I do," she said. "I want to be free."

Afterward, we sat together and she told me her story. Twelve years earlier, her husband had left her and moved in with another woman. She felt constantly irritated, physically ill and, on most days, her thoughts centered on his betrayal, despite the years that had passed.

In her mind, forgiving him was an act he didn't deserve. She realized how unforgiveness toward her ex-husband had trapped her, but it seemed impossible to move on, despite the fact that the results of unforgiving were just as debilitating as the original offense, and the offender was nowhere in sight.

I asked her if she was willing to offer her emotions, her pain and her ex-husband to God. She was more than willing. She was ready. God's presence was tangible as she lifted up the burden that had kept her stuck for 12 years.

Since then, we have stayed in touch, and she continues to live a forgiving lifestyle. The major benefit is that she is tuned in to what God has for her today instead of what was taken from her yesterday. Her ex-husband has no idea of her transformation.

He's been out of the picture for a long time. But this wasn't about him . . . not really; because none of us have the power to change another human being.

Perhaps you are also struggling with the concept of forgiveness. Have you ever said or asked,

Why should I forgive? I did nothing wrong.

Doesn't forgiveness let the offender off the hook? How is that fair?

I forgave someone and he or she was not remorseful.

I will change when he or she does.

These are compelling statements, and they are understandable in situations that require forgiving someone. But do you notice that these words center on the actions of others? At some point, we recognize our own need. Whether anyone else is willing to change or not, we are tired of feeling stuck emotionally and spiritually.

In Mark 10:51-52, we read of a blind man named Bartimaeus who heard a crowd approach. When Bartimaeus realized who was within reach, he wouldn't be silenced. He began to call out the name of Jesus.

"What do you want me to do for you?" Jesus asked him.

The blind man said, "Rabbi, I want to see."

Jesus stopped everything to open the eyes of this man, and his life was so changed by that encounter that he followed Christ alongside the road.

Are you crying out to God today? Are you shouting, "I want to be free of these feelings . . . I want to forgive"?

God hears that cry.

Where do you begin your journey toward freedom? Let's start with an understanding of the foundation of forgiveness.

סָלַח translated *salach* [Hebrew]: (1) to give up resentment of or a claim to requital for; (2) to pardon; (3) to grant relief from payment of; (4) to cease to feel resentment.

WHAT IS FORGIVENESS?

Forgiveness is an intentional act to let go of the burden and restrictions of bitterness, anger, rage or unresolved emotions connected to a person or event. In other words, forgiveness is surrender. It's offering up resentment. It's giving up the desire to punish. It's letting go of anger. It's getting out of the "debt collection" business.

In Luke 5:18-26, we read of a full house of people who had come from all around the region to hear Jesus teach. A paralyzed man's friends carried him on a mat to that location. They had heard that Jesus was a healer, and they trekked across Galilee to find Him. The crowd was so huge that the men carrying the paralyzed man couldn't push through. So they climbed onto the roof and took off some tiles. Ingenious, right? They lowered their friend through the roof, right in front of Jesus.

The man's physical need was apparent, but Jesus said something surprising: "When Jesus saw their faith, he said, 'Friend, your sins are forgiven'" (Luke 5:20).

Were the friends confused by Jesus' words? Maybe. The Pharisees sitting there certainly were. They could only see the obvious physical impairment.

On hearing that his sins were forgiven, the paralyzed man could have called it a day. "Take me home, this guy hasn't got a clue." But he surrendered to Jesus. Even though he could have argued that the real problem was his legs, he followed Jesus' instructions. In faith, he jumped to his feet, picked up his mat and danced all the way home as he praised God.

Jesus saw the whole man. He started from the inside out.

How many times do we bring the obvious to God?

Lord, she hurt me.

God, I can't sleep.

I'm angry and I yell at my kids. Make it stop.

I don't feel like a Christian.

How many times does God look beyond what is in plain sight to the heart issue? He does it every time.

People don't do this. In most cases, they define you as broken or point out your anger issue or tell you to get on with it.

Seeing the whole person is a compassionate act of a Savior who knows us best. When He reveals the root of our problem, we have a choice. We can continue to plead with Him about the obvious problems, or we can surrender.

In a sense, we pick up our mats. Instead of letting unforgiveness keep us tethered and sick, we allow God to begin the process of making us whole.

How Do You Forgive?

To surrender is to offer God a willing heart. You don't offer the issue, the other person, the obvious symptoms.

You offer yourself.

You offer up your thoughts, your feelings and your woundedness to God and acknowledge that you can't do it on your own. This is an ultimate act of surrender. In James 4:7-8, we are instructed, "submit yourselves, then, to God" (v. 7). That is a vulnerable act as you give God access to every area of your heart. You hold up the past; you trust Him with today; and you have hope for tomorrow.

Surrender to God is an active form of spiritual warfare, because you are no longer battling alone. With God's help, you are resisting the enemy who desires nothing more than to rob you of purpose and joy. The enemy has no choice but to step back when you follow this precept: "Come near to God and he will come near to you" (v. 8).

Are you willing to surrender?

Think about what Jesus told the lame man.

Stand: Put down all your beliefs that you can do it on your own. Put down your excuses and your failed attempts. Stop waiting for someone else to change first.

When you stand, suddenly things are different. You are no longer mired in a crowd of sick people. You see a new horizon and recognize the possibilities beyond the limited view of just a few moments before.

Pick up your mat: Mentally hold up your heart to God. Hold nothing back. Invite Him into every chamber. Every thought.

Every hurt. He's not afraid of your true feelings. He's seen them all along.

When you pick up your mat, you pick up those things that seemed like protection. Yes, the mat kept you off the cold, hard ground, but you can only go as far as the mat will take you. Resentment, anger, perfectionism, fear, addiction, control—these are only a few things that can comprise your mat.

When you pick up your mat, you are saying to God that you desire to go where He wants to take you rather than stay limited. That you trust He'll be your protector rather than a defense mechanism.

Walk: It's not about how strong you are. It's about His love for you, and the power of God that is so tangible that He offers His "glorious, unlimited resources . . . [to] empower you with inner strength through his Spirit" (Eph. 3:16, *NLT*). We walk as we follow Jesus. Step by step. Hour by hour. Day by day.

When you first stand after being crippled by unforgiveness or anger or hurt, it won't feel natural at first. It may even feel painful. You may want to reach for your mat. You might even plop down on that mat for a moment.

Instead of giving in to those feelings, just walk.

Like my granddaughter, Elle, your first steps might be tentative. She took forever to walk. She *could* walk, but she didn't know it yet. She walked with confidence when she held on to objects like the coffee table, the wall or even just the fingertip of an adult. But the moment her safety net was out of reach, she swayed. Suddenly, everything was different. Scary. She plopped to her diapered bottom and wailed. She had tasted freedom, but she also wasn't ready to let go and walk solo. Twelve months passed. Fourteen. Sixteen. Seventeen. Honestly, there were times that we wondered if she'd ever take her first solo step. We cheered on each small move toward independence, all the while knowing that one day she would have to let go and walk. It was up to her.

That's what it looks like when we start to doubt.

If I were strong, I wouldn't feel this way. I wouldn't waver. Why can't I do this?

Like my beautiful blonde, blue-eyed grandbaby, it's not how well you walk from day one, but that you took the first step. Just as I held my arms out, and my face lit up with joy at her courage, God sees those painful first steps. He also knows with certainty that one day you will walk with skill and even run.

It was nearly 17 months when Elle took her first steps alone. We were celebrating Christmas with family. She stood beside me, her tiny fingers pinching my jeans. Then she released the fabric. She looked toward the dining room where all her favorite people laughed around the table. She took one step. Then another. I held my breath and tried not to rejoice out loud as she walked across the room like a shaky old man.

It was a beautiful sight.

Once she experienced what freedom really felt like, she pushed away our hands when we tried to help her over a raised step or as she transitioned from hard floor to carpet. She had figured it out! Yes, letting go seems impossible until you actually do it and discover what is beyond your comfort zone.

Praise: When you are willing to forgive, you are not only allowing God to see the junk inside, but you are also in the process of being "made complete" (Eph. 3:19, *NLT*). You are surprised when you turn a corner and realize that a part of your heart has been unburdened, or you start to see a person or event in a different light.

The obvious healing may not yet be apparent to the world, but on the inside you know that God is at work.

Praise is a choice when you feel wobbly or fall down. It's the words that come out of your mouth even on those days when the mat beckons and calls you to return to familiar territory. You praise God because healing isn't a single act. It's a series of miracles as you choose to stand, to pick up your mat, to walk and to worship Him as Christ delves below the obvious impairment to lead you in a new direction.

Why Do We Forgive?

Sometimes I want to wave a flag with the word "freedom" blazed on it to share with those who are in a rut of anger or hurt, or who continue in damaging patterns that keep wounds fresh and open, that there's another way.

Forgiveness is liberty. It cuts all the ties that prevent you from discovering who you were intended to be from the very beginning. It lightens the baggage you've been carrying. It opens your eyes to the opportunities around you.

Living a forgiving lifestyle doesn't change the past; that's impossible. But it absolutely transforms you and alters the story of your future and those you love.

Now that we know what forgiveness is, let's explore what forgiveness is not.

FORGIVENESS IS NOT ALLOWING ABUSE TO CONTINUE

Perhaps you have been told that forgiving means that you turn the other cheek (it does, and later we'll explore what this powerful verse in Scripture means), or you are encouraged to remain in a situation that leaves you or your children open to abuse because "if you forgive, you won't leave" or "you are supposed to submit."

As believers of the Bible, it's key that we quote and live out Scripture within its context. This means that we study God's Word in light of when it was said, where it was said, why it was said and to whom it was said, taking into consideration the cultural nuances of that time, and then apply the spiritual and practical implications for today. We study the whole Word of God, not just scraps and pieces. We compare Scripture with Scripture to ensure that we are holding it in the proper light. We do this so that we don't build standalone doctrines that contradict the heart and majority of biblical teachings.

For example, let's look at the character of Jesus, using His own words to reveal His heart toward abuse.

In John 8:3-9, Jesus held back the men from striking an adulterous woman with stones, saying, "Let any one of you who is without sin be the first to throw a stone at her" (v. 7).

In Luke 18:15-17, Jesus held children in His lap when they ran to Him, and He scolded the disciples for trying to push them away, saying, "Let the little children come to me, and do not hinder them, for the kingdom of God belongs to such as these" (v. 16).

In Matthew 25:35-45, He taught His disciples to feed the poor, give water to the thirsty and visit those who were in shackles, saying, "whatever you did for one of the least of these brothers and sisters of mine, you did for me" (v. 40).

These are only a few of the numerous Scripture passages that reveal a Savior who stood up for those who are abused or at the mercy of others.

We also find Jesus pointing out how narrowly defined religious interpretations can keep us from understanding the full intent of the law (see Matt. 12:1-13).

This can also happen when Ephesians 5:22-23 is quoted out of context, and women are instructed to remain in abusive situations, labeling it as forgiving. "Wives, submit yourselves to your own husbands as you do to the Lord" (v. 22) completely changes in tone when you leave out verses 25-31 of Ephesians 5, where Paul encourages men to love their wives as Jesus loved the Church, giving Himself up for it, and to love their wives as their own bodies. This is a sacrificial love that never demands its own way or bends another to its will through abuse.

In the case of abuse, too many have remained in a situation where a spouse is repeatedly unfaithful or where they or their children were physically harmed because a well-intentioned person said, "Just forgive," and offered Scripture taken out of context or too narrowly defined.

If a person is destructive, abusive or his or her actions put you or your family in harm's way, there *is* hope for forgiveness and even reconciliation. However, forgiveness that transforms, in this instance, begins as you set appropriate boundaries that allow you to work toward the healthiest relationship possible.

But Doesn't God Call Us to Love Unconditionally?

The answer is yes. The Father loves us so much that He led Christ to the cross where He bore our sin—the weight of every murderous thought, every treacherous act, every transgression, every sin that was and is to come. Afterwards, He sought us with intent, drawing us to the cross to find forgiveness and a relationship with the Father.

Soon after Jesus began His adult ministry, it was reported that "from that time on Jesus began to preach, 'Repent, for the kingdom of heaven has come near'" (Matt. 4:17).

From that time on . . .

That means from that moment until now, repentance was Jesus' message. The word "repent" in its truest sense means to "change your mind." This change of mind leads to a change of heart, which takes you down a new road. It is at the cross that you acknowledge your sadness over wrongs inflicted. It is at the cross where you begin to see your relationship with God in a new light. You respond differently. You listen with renewed insight because a relationship has been forged.

Often, Christians focus on the unconditional love of God, yet fail to pair it with the call to repentance. This can lead them to counsel the abused to try to out-forgive God as they offer the unrepentant free license to continue to harm, violate, abuse or inflict injury, and deem it scriptural.

Leslie Vernick, a licensed Christian counselor and speaker, wrote:

> Jesus tells us that there is nothing more important than to learn how to love God and others well (see Matt. 22:36-39). Because people are so important to God, He warns us about the painful consequences of destructive relationship patterns.[1]

Vernick goes on to describe the damage to relationships, like a house slowly destroyed due to termite or mold damage, producing relationships that are crushed, stifled, suppressed, shattered, demolished or broken by the sinful relationship patterns, and opposite of God's plan according to Scripture of how to love and treat each other.[2]

Let's balance this. It's not saying that a person has to conform to our way of thinking, or apologize or change according to the way we think they should.

It's not saying that we withhold forgiveness until a person meets our standards of righteous living, or even until they change.

It doesn't mean holding forgiveness like a carrot on a stick, demanding that a person earn our love or say the right words, or pay back word for word or action for action what he or she has done wrong.

We read in Colossians 3:13, "Forgive as the Lord forgave you." God's grace is immeasurable. God's gift of the cross and transformation is unmatched. We *do* heal as we forgive and let go, whether that person desires to repent or not. But just as God calls each of us to repentance (see Col. 3:5-10), He wants the same for the person who has offended you. He loves that person, right where he or she is—stuck in sin or mixed-up thinking.

In the case of abuse, when it is allowed to continue, or when we allow evil to run rampant and call it forgiveness, there is little chance for transformation unless that person hits a brick wall of his own making.

How, then, do you forgive like Jesus?

You forgive like Jesus by living at peace with all, so far as it depends on you (see Rom. 12:18). We forgive like Jesus by praying for that person; by loving him or her, if even from a distance; and by keeping a door open to reconciliation as repentance occurs.

We also get rid of malice and anger in our own heart. We let the Holy Spirit examine our life for those areas where God wants to move in (see Rom. 12:7-21).

READY TO TAKE THIS DEEPER?

Now that we know what forgiveness is and what it is not, let's begin to explore in the next few chapters the diverse meanings of forgiveness found in Scripture. I studied the word "forgive" for months. At that time, I did so for my own benefit. I had struggled with the concept of a one-size-fits all forgiveness for some time.

What if someone dings your car door with a shopping cart? *Just forgive.*

How do you live a normal life when a relative has molested you? *Just forgive.*

What if a controlling parent refuses to let go and it's hurting your marriage? *Just forgive.*

I understood the power of forgiveness and that God commands us to do it. I embraced the concept of forgiving as a gift both received and one that I could offer others. But what I hoped to discover was more... and I did.

Nestled under the umbrella of the word "forgive" in both the Old and New Testaments is a host of rich words and meanings that lead to deeper knowledge of why it is so important to God, as well as practical application that you and I can put into effect in real life. These meanings help us understand why we forgive and how we forgive and what it means to forgive, and what forgiveness really means in all types of relationships and situations. Scripture shows us that it is possible to forgive where we cannot forgive in our own power. It reveals the treasures we receive as we apply forgiveness in our everyday lives.

I discovered that in the Old Testament, forgiveness is primarily focused on God's need to forgive (pardon) those He loves. In the New Testament, grace is introduced, and the focus shifts to include our need to receive forgiveness and to give it to each other. Jesus placed great emphasis on forgiving as a result of a changed heart and knowing God in a personal manner.

As we study forgiveness together, you'll discover that every meaning may not apply to you or your situation today, but forgiving is not a once-in-a-lifetime opportunity. This teaching will help you when you encounter that person, that word, that situation, and you need to remind yourself of what God offers you so that you can live free.

In addition, though a story may be about infidelity, and that is not exactly your story as well, we all experience unfaithfulness at some point, whether through a broken friendship or a relationship we trusted that let us down. The story simply introduces a real person who has struggled through a real problem to find resolution or hope.

Now, before we begin our deeper study, you have an opportunity to take what you've learned so far and get alone with God to consider it. Take your time. There are no right answers. This is simply your first act of surrender as you invite God to join you in the process.

JUST YOU AND GOD

1. Which of the following definitions define the burden that you currently carry?

   a. resentment
   b. a need for justice or revenge
   c. thoughts and actions tied to the past that affect me and my current relationships
   d. a desire to change whether anyone else changes or not

2. Read Matthew 11:28-30. In this invitation, Jesus offers a promise. Write a prayer that reflects your desire to rest from your burden.

   _____

   _____

   _____

   _____

3. What obvious impairment resulting from unforgiveness in your life can you or others see? (It can be anger, or the inability to trust, or perfectionism or a host of other symptoms of unforgiveness.)

   _____

   _____

   _____

   _____

4. God sees beneath the obvious to the heart of the daughter He loves. What do you believe He sees that needs to be made whole?

_____

_____

_____

_____

_____

5. The first step to living in forgiveness is to surrender. Forget charting a success strategy or starting a to-do list; you simply give to God what is bigger than you. What are you willing to surrender in this moment?

_____

_____

_____

_____

6. "Surrendering is an active form of spiritual warfare, because you are no longer battling alone. With God's help, you are resisting the enemy who desires nothing more than to rob you of purpose and joy." What were your thoughts as you read that statement? How does it apply to you today?

_____

_____

_____

_____

7. Read 2 Corinthians 3:17-18. The word "transformed" in this passage means a spiritual inner change. If no one but you changes in this journey to forgive, what do you stand to gain regardless of any other person's inability to change?

_____

_____

_____

_____

8. In what ways did this chapter change your definition of forgiveness?

_____

_____

_____

_____

_____

SALACH PRINCIPLE

Surrender to God the burden and restrictions of unforgiveness.

TO *SALACH* FORGIVE
Surrender

PRAYER

*Father, I offer every wounded place in my heart and my thoughts.
I thank You that Your strength becomes mine as we walk this path
together. I am excited to see where an unburdened heart
will lead me with Your help.*

Notes
1. Leslie Vernick, *The Emotionally Destructive Relationship* (Eugene, OR: Harvest House, 2007), p. 12.
2. Ibid.

PART 2

What we Gain
When we Forgive

You Leave One Place to Go to Another

*Forgiveness is the key that unlocks the door of resentment
and the handcuffs of hatred.*

Corrie ten Boom, *Clippings from My Notebook*

When Karen was seven years old, she knew that the word "alcoholic" described her father. He was like Dr. Jekyll and Mr. Hyde. One moment he hurt the people he loved; the next moment he was sorry. It's true that he was gregarious and well liked. He was a business owner and respected in the community; but the monster in the bottle brought out a completely different side.

He left his family when Karen was in second grade, only to return and then leave again when she was in fifth grade. His absence left her mother angry and bitter, and she reminded her children often of what their father did wrong. She told them about his affairs and about the money he spent on women and drinking.

Karen bore the weight of her mother's words, but also of her father's choice. Their small home looked normal from the outside, but on the inside it was clear there wasn't enough money to go around. She wanted to invite friends over, but she was ashamed of what they would see.

In high school, and her first year of college, Karen tried not to have a relationship with her dad. It was difficult to do when you worked for your dad. She needed money for tuition, so she worked at his catering company. She was there physically, but she checked out emotionally.

In her junior year of high school, she became a Christian, but her new beliefs only complicated her relationship with her father. When she prayed about it, she told God she would forgive her father, but only when he asked her personally. She was growing to understand that forgiving was key to letting go of her past. She realized how much grace Christ had showed her over and over when she least deserved it. The tug on her heart to forgive wouldn't leave.

One day, she found her dad asleep in his chair at work. He had a glass of alcohol in his hand and a lighted cigarette charring the desk. She stood there, shaking. And then the nudging inside came again, and for the first time, she didn't resist it. She rubbed out the smoldering cigarette and left a note on his desk. It read: *I love you, Dad.*

Weeks passed, but there was no response to her note. It hurt that he said nothing, but she resolved to love her father.

She didn't expect him to give what he couldn't or wouldn't provide. She wasn't asking God to reconcile their relationship or to change her father. She wasn't trying to out-love God. She was simply letting go out of love for God.

Later that year, her father fell and was seriously injured. He had broken his back and wasn't found for 72 hours. In that vulnerable space of time, all he could do was think about his life. In the darkness of that small room he asked God to forgive him. Later, after his rescue, he decided to stop drinking. He went to all the people he had hurt, including his daughter, and asked for forgiveness.

What if he hadn't been injured? What if he hadn't faced his mortality and changed his ways?

When her father finally asked for her forgiveness, Karen had already begun the process. She had forgiven him despite his lack of remorse, his continued behavior and his lack of response to her note. These were things he was not willing to offer at that time, but she did it for her own sake and because her God had called her to forgive.

LEAVING ONE PLACE TO FIND ANOTHER

Karen didn't gloss over the ache of her father's neglect and abandonment ever since she was a child, but she found compassion—an unlikely benefit that surprised her. As Karen shared her story her voice broke, though not in the places I expected. She cried when she told me her father confessed that for years he felt beyond the reach of grace.

Aphiemi is one of the most common words that surfaces when speaking of forgiveness. It is a Greek word that means to let go, to give up a debt, to forgive, to remit or to hurl away. But the most powerful interpretation of this word is this: *to leave one place to go to another*.

When we forgive, we leave anger to find joy. We leave hatred to find love. We leave dysfunction to find stability. We leave judgment to find compassion. We leave our identity of a neglected child to walk into our identity as God's child, filled with purpose and pursuing all that He has been waiting for us to experience.

fiðhai [Greek] translated *aphiemi:* (1) to send away; (2) to let it die; (3) to exchange it for something else; (4) to give up a debt; (5) to forgive.

STOP TO WORK THINGS OUT

Jesus' words in Matthew 5:24-25 explain what to do if you have discord with another person. He says that if you are offering a gift at the altar, and you remember that a brother has something against you, leave your gift there and "go and be reconciled to them" (v. 24). Then you are free to come back and offer your gift. The *MESSAGE* rewords this last part in an interesting way: "then, come back and work things out with God."

Jesus was telling the disciples to stop what they were doing and leave their gift at the altar because, just as in Karen's case, He cared more about the disciples' wellbeing than their sacrifice.

When Karen forgave her father, his attention was elsewhere—on alcohol, on women, on his business and on his reputation in the community. Reconciliation wasn't possible at that time.

So what did God know that Karen did not?

When you have been neglected or abandoned, it can demolish your view of God. You might strive to please Him but think it's impossible. You may live in fear of the hammer striking at any moment. Perhaps you struggle with the concept of unconditional love, and a heavenly father figure that is supposed to protect you may produce anger rather than comfort.

This can be carried into your personal life. It looks different for each of us, but it can be debilitating in our relationships.

The God who Karen befriended had better things for her, and if she remained stalled in unforgiveness she might not discover how to think differently, how to give her children stability, how to love without fear of abandonment and so much more.

When Karen forgave (hurled it away), she left behind her childhood to fully step into her role as an adult. She was no longer tied to resentment, bitterness and futility due to her father's decisions. She was not responsible to wipe her father's (or any person's) slate clean of wrongdoing. Only Christ can do that through His finished work on the cross.

Karen's gesture was simply a gift she offered her father. It was not her responsibility to force him to take it or acknowledge it. When she let go, she found a higher path waiting for her.

This is why God loves us enough to command us to forgive.

If you were neglected due to a loved one's addiction, or other reasons, this command may stir raw emotions. Every person deserves to know that he or she is loved. If you didn't know that, what do you do now?

ACCEPT "WHAT IS"

Karen's father wasn't beyond help, but it had to be his choice. We read in Matthew 15:14 that Jesus encountered a group of religious men. They were angry because Jesus wasn't teaching about ceremonial washing or showing which foods to avoid. They were confrontational, which frustrated the disciples. "What are you going to do, Jesus?" they asked.

Jesus instructed them to let the Pharisees go. There's that word again. The root word of "let them go" is *aphiemi*.

Let them go. Move on. They are blind. If the blind follow the blind, they'll fall into a pit. Are you going to follow them into the pit?

Jesus didn't condemn the religious men for their blindness. The men were attached to their traditions. By commanding His followers to let them alone, He wasn't asking them to not care about their blindness. He was reminding His disciples that they could not make a person who thinks he has 20/20 vision understand that he is blind.

When Karen forgave her father, it was a time of spiritual and emotional growth for her. She started to see herself as more than the daughter of an alcoholic. She was no longer the little girl who couldn't have friends over because she was embarrassed. She started to see new possibilities.

The addiction continued to affect her father, but the hold was released over her. She accepted the reality of his situation as she focused on moving forward.

LOVE FROM AFAR

Where there is addiction or self-destructive behavior, we often must love from a distance. But Karen worked with her father. They were in proximity several days a week. Due to the alcoholism, it was challenging to love her father up close and personal; but as her heart began to change, she chose to love him from afar.

This looked very different from her first decision, which was to not love him at all.

What does loving someone from a distance look like in real life? You pray for that person, but you don't try to fix him when he isn't ready. You ask God to reveal His love through you, but you don't cushion the person from the consequences of his or her actions.

You pray for compassion to love the person in his brokenness, and the strength not to live in brokenness with him.

You often hear that you can't change anyone but yourself, and that is truth. But may I take that one step further? Sometimes our own transformation can seem just as impossible a task. That's why responding to God's call to forgive is such an act of strength. Forgiving someone doesn't say that you are in the wrong, as some believe. It says that you are no longer willing to remain mired in the pit of unforgiveness.

You want more from life—for yourself and for those you love who have nothing to do with the past; and in order to do that, you are willing to take a step in the opposite direction from where you've been headed.

RESOLVE THE SITUATION IN YOUR OWN HEART

What do you do if you are changing and the other person is not? Charles Stanley, in *The Gift of Forgiveness*, suggests placing two chairs opposite each other and imagining the other person sitting in that chair. He suggests that you disclose everything that was done to harm you, without holding back your emotions or tears.[1] By doing this you put a face on where you've been. This is what affected me. This is my history.

But it also provides a mile marker of sorts. This is where I was, and this is where I want to go next.

This openness allows you to begin to resolve the situation in your own heart.

But don't stop there. This is where you need God the most. You have cracked open a vault long closed, loosing thoughts and emotions long held back. God isn't afraid of that, nor is He turned away by those emotions.

One of the women who came alongside me as I wrote this book revealed secrets she had only told a best friend. As she spoke to that empty chair, for the first time she talked about what had taken place and how that one incident changed the way she viewed herself and the way she thought God saw her. She felt she was damaged forever.

It was an honest, breathtakingly beautiful moment.

By mentally placing the person across from her in that chair, she was free to say the things she had pushed down. This woman had resolved to keep her secrets and her thoughts to herself, but the pain of staying in the same place, going in the same direction, was a constant reminder that it wasn't working. She wasn't sure where honesty would take her, but she invited God into that moment, asking Him to show her the next step, and the next after that.

As you resolve the situation in your own heart, it's very possible that the person will, as in Karen's case, respond as you forgive and change; but the reality is that there are people who will take years to change their ways. Some may find help due to a life-altering crisis like jail or a health scare. Others won't understand why you want them to change. And some may never change.

But you keep growing.

My biological father is dead. He was never a father to me or to my older sister. I can't change that abandonment. It is what it is. But I can learn from it. I can grow in spite of it. I can be a mom who loves her children and grandchildren like crazy. I can apologize or work through conflict when there is discord with someone I love. I can believe that there are no boundaries on how much I can love and relate to the people in my life who matter.

Will there be a happy ending in your relationship? The hope is always that yes, there will; but regardless of the answer, will you consider inviting the Holy Spirit to tenderly expose and heal the bruised areas of your heart?

GETTING OUT OF THE DEBT COLLECTION BUSINESS

Today, people often comment on Karen's relationship with her father. "You're so lucky," they say.

When that happens, Karen thinks about the first half of her life. It was not what she hoped it would be, but it's also something she cannot change. She could live in the land of "what-ifs." What if her father had changed earlier? What if she hadn't had to go through hard times as a girl? Instead she focuses on what she has now. Her father never attended any of her games, but he doesn't miss his grandchildren's events. He didn't serve the Lord when she was a teen, but he takes her children to a bench in her backyard where he shares his love for God with them, tears pouring down his face as he shares the reality of God's immense grace.

To *aphiemi* forgive, we give up a debt and exchange it for something else. We begin by first understanding that every person has a different camera angle. If you ask five bystanders to describe the same accident, no one person will see it in the same way. Each person sees it through his or her unique lens. Where the person was standing. What he or she was doing at the time. How it affected him or her personally.

Perhaps until this moment you've only looked at a person or a past event through your perspective. Take a step back for a moment. What was the situation or circumstances at the time from the other person's point of view? What influences led the person to that place? How does this knowledge change the way you see that person or a past event? It may change nothing, but it does add dimension.

Second, as you let go of old debts, understand that there is an appropriate time and way to discuss old hurts. Did you know that holidays are often the most explosive time to do that? We have such high expectations that we may experience meltdown because the day is nothing like we hoped, or it brings back old memories, and that's the exact moment we try to fix everything that has gone wrong. Nothing or nobody can live up to our hopes for that day.

Talking about hard topics at an appropriate time gives you both the opportunity to address the real issues between you. Your point of view will be different, due to time and circumstances, as will the other person's. Pray about it before you talk. Pray together, if that is possible. Ask God to be an honored guest. As you talk, don't forget to share what you see that is good, and affirm the growth and lessons learned, and the impact upon you.

Third, as an adult, be realistic about the other person's growth. Paint a new picture that includes all the years that have passed. Who is he or she now? What are the possibilities for your relationship today? Be truthful about his or her shortcomings, but also about your own. Are you willing to celebrate the baby steps each of you have taken?

Finally, is there anything you need to let go of so that you can go in a new direction? Is there hostility, anger or high expectations that are impossible to meet? Remember that normal doesn't mean perfect. Not for that person, and not for you. Not even in relationships that seem to have it all together. This thing called family, even in the best of situations, can be complicated at times. We love each other. We believe the best about each other unless we prove otherwise. We work through conflict with grace and honesty, and we take responsibility when we say or do something we wish we hadn't.

My Story Has a Different Ending Than Karen's

What if the person who neglected or abandoned you hasn't had a change of heart? How does *aphiemi* forgiving cut the ties to the pain of neglect in these instances?

We read in Luke 7:36-50 that Jesus was at the home of a good man named Simon. While they were eating, a woman enters the house. This isn't unusual, as Jesus is an honored guest, and many have come to meet him.

But this woman is the town prostitute.

She kneels at Jesus' feet and weeps; then she dries her tears that have fallen on His feet with her hair. She pours perfume over His calloused, road-weary feet and kisses them. Simon, the host, stands by, confused.

Why is this person in my home?

Why doesn't Jesus push her away?

Does He not realize what kind of woman is touching Him?

Jesus looks up at His host who has said nothing audibly at this point and remarks, "Simon, I have something to tell you. . . . Two people owed money to a certain moneylender. One owed him five hundred denarii [a denarius was the usual daily wage of a day laborer], and the other fifty. Neither of them had the money to pay him back, so he forgave the debts of both. Now which of them will love him more?"

Simon replies, "I suppose the one who had the bigger debt forgiven."

"You have judged correctly," Jesus says.

Then he turns toward the woman and says to Simon, "Do you see this woman? I came into your house. You did not give me any water for my feet, but she wet my feet with her tears and wiped them with her hair. You did not give me a kiss, but this woman, from the time I entered, has not stopped kissing my feet. You did not put oil on my head, but she has poured perfume on my feet. Therefore, I tell you, her many sins have been forgiven—as her great love has shown. But whoever has been forgiven little loves little."

Then Jesus says to her, "Your sins are forgiven" (see vv. 40-48).

We often romanticize stories from the Bible, but let's put ourselves there for a moment. Somewhere there is a family whose daughter had turned to prostitution. It's not what they hoped for their daughter. It has brought shame on their family. They hide their heads when their daughter's name is mentioned.

Perhaps there are abandoned children—not an unlikely thought due to her circumstances and the time period. What do they think of their mom? What shame do they carry? How many times have they cried themselves to sleep? What do the other children in the synagogue have to say about their mom?

This woman cannot walk through the streets without her neighbors crossing to the other side, pulling the hems of their robes away so that she will not soil them. She stands at a distance at noon while all the other women gather at the well, talking and laughing. She waits until they leave so that she can fill her bucket without their condemnation or gossip.

Simon has opened his home and put on the best feast for Jesus, his honored guest, and yet this woman dares to boldly walk across the threshold of his home and intimately touch the Master.

She's a bad person. She should know better than to think she deserves mercy. She should change/could change/needs to change. Everybody knows that. How can the Master not see it?

If your mom or dad or spouse or caregiver is like that woman, you might very well feel the same as Simon.

We don't know what led that woman to become the town prostitute; but what we do know is that she somehow hoped that Jesus might love her in her brokenness.

In many cases where a person is addicted or in bondage, it is hard to turn away from the image in the mirror that says, "You are sick; you have wasted your life; your choices affect those you love; you are not worthy of love."

These people can drink more or numb themselves further with substances; and when they wake up, there's just more carnage to remind them of the people they've become.

After her father's conversion, Karen later discovered that he used to pray repeatedly for mercy. The day she left a note was a tangible sign that perhaps God had heard his prayers.

To *aphiemi* love in this passage in Luke 7 is to heed a call from God's heart that loves those who cannot love themselves. We've already discussed what forgiveness isn't and the practicalities that come with loving someone whose destructive choices are affecting themselves and others. But this is a conscious choice that hears the knocking on the heart that says, "love me."

It's hard to grasp so great a love, isn't it? Oswald Chambers once said, "It is possible to take the forgiveness of sin, the gift of the Holy Ghost, and our sanctification with the simplicity of faith, and to forget at what enormous cost to God it was all made ours."[2]

We've received that kind of forgiveness, but how do we offer it to another? Like Simon, our efforts aren't the focus of this story. To *aphiemi* forgive we acknowledge that this person, with debt so deep that a lifetime of apologies won't suffice, is valuable to God.

It's a shift in perspective that opens the door wide enough to see that person in a different way. We aren't responsible to pardon the person or change him or her, that's God's job. But we become more like our heavenly Father as we let compassion tiptoe in.

JUST YOU AND GOD

1. Are you willing to accept that "it is what it is"?" How does that change things?

2. How do you identify with Karen's story?

3. What does it mean to you to love from a distance? How does this differ from what you are currently doing?

4. When you read Matthew 5:40 and Matthew 6:14, what is your reaction? What is one tangible step you can take in response to these commandments?

5. Mentally place your offender in a chair. Write down all the things you need to say to this person. Be honest. Once you have

shared your thoughts, it is important that you invite God to sit with you in the conversation. Ask Him to help you let go so that you can live without those emotions that tie you to this person or event.

_____

_____

_____

_____

_____

_____

6. What does it mean to you to "leave one place to go to another"?

_____

_____

_____

_____

7. In what ways have you been in the debt collection business? How has that affected you or your loved ones?

_____

_____

_____

_____

8. "To _aphiemi_ forgive we acknowledge that this person, with debt so deep that a lifetime of apologies won't suffice, is valuable to God." Share your thoughts on this statement.

_____

_____

_____

_____

APHIEMI PRINCIPLE
Let go and move in a new direction.

TO APHIEMI FORGIVE
Get out of the debt collection business.

PRAYER
Father, I realize there are places I cannot go and things I cannot see when tied to the past or another person. Thank You for leading me in a new direction. Today, I pray for this person who has such a great debt. I thank You that no person is beyond your reach.

Notes
1. Charles Stanley, *The Gift of Forgiveness* (Nashville, TN: Thomas Nelson, 2002), p. 173.
2. Oswald Chambers, *My Utmost for His Highest* (Grand Rapids, MI: Discovery House Publishers, 1993).

3

God Moves In

You may have to declare your forgiveness a hundred times the first day and the second day, but the third day will be less and each day after, until one day you will realize that you have forgiven completely.

William P. Young, *The Shack*

Carlie lay in the fetal position,[1] tissues piled in a crumpled mess around her. Her Bible and devotion book rested on the thick carpet beside her. She had been crying out to God all morning after she felt God speak to her heart these words:

Forgive him. You need to forgive.

It had only been three days since her husband had walked out of their marriage of nearly 30 years and away from her and their grown children and the life they had built together. He left all of this to be with another woman. Carlie had discovered that he had built a secret life with this woman for months, and perhaps even years.

And now God was asking her to forgive him?

How do you forgive when your husband has been sleeping with someone? How do you forgive when the life you thought you had is in shambles? How do you forgive when you are lying on an examination table with tears flowing, humiliated, as you are tested for possible STDs you never realized you were exposed to until now?

As a believer, Carlie instinctively understood that at some point she would be asked to forgive, but this was too soon. She was a mess of raw nerves. Tears came without warning at the most unexpected times, and they were not only unwelcome but unnerving.

Carlie ate because she knew she should, but it didn't stay with her. Her normally low blood pressure was high. She hadn't slept since discovering her husband's secret.

That morning, she held her clutched tissues in the air, saying, "God, You're not being fair, and You are asking too much." She deserved more time to grieve, more time to be angry with her husband and more time to replay possible payback scenarios in her mind. The last thing she wanted to hear from God was about forgiveness, so she asked God to understand that she was in pain and that her husband should be asking her for forgiveness, not the other way around.

Carlie, not only do I want you to forgive, but I want you to pray for blessings in his life.

At that, Carlie stomped out of the room, saying out loud, "That's it. Devotions and prayer time is over for today. I'm walking away from this ridiculous request. I'm exhausted, and my lack of sleep is messing with my mind. God, you love me too much to make such a request."

Every day she heard the same words gently whispered during her devotions time. She pushed them away. She continued to lay in bed awake at night. She continued to lose weight.

Her children were hurting, though they reacted in different ways. Her son stepped up as a protector, trying to shield his mother and his sister; Carlie's daughter was not afraid to pose the tough questions about her father.

As days passed, Carlie decided to tell extended family and very close friends the news. Each day after Carlie went to the office, she avoided the kind words or touches or any sign of sympathy from friends or co-workers. Hugs were definitely dangerous; they could demolish her barely-held-together exterior.

I Didn't Do Anything Wrong

Why would a loving God ask Carlie to forgive, especially so soon after she suffered her loss? She didn't know what to do with the word "separation," and divorce had never been a consideration.

Her marriage wasn't perfect, but she and her husband had been working on it. In fact, their counseling sessions had offered glimmers of hope. They had often talked about the next season of their lives. They had celebrated their children's marriages and loved the role they played in their in-law children's lives. They looked forward to the joy of becoming grandparents one day.

The secrets Carlie discovered that fateful morning only affirmed that despite their conversations about the future, she had been living with a stranger for a long time. All the things that once described Carlie's life—security, a complete family unit, family vacations, time around the table laughing, her husband's arms around her just days before she discovered his secret affair—were gone.

Her husband had made a choice to be unfaithful—to walk away from all that God had given him. The one unchangeable fact in this mess was her love for God and God's love for her and her family. Despite her husband's choices, God and His promises over her life and her children's had not changed. He was still her strength. He was still Lord of her present and future. He was still her shelter.

In spite of that, her husband's hurtful actions were a perfect invitation for a host of unwanted and destructive emotions to walk into her heart and take up residence. To be honest, it made sense. Who could blame her? She could have found any number of people who would have agreed that not only was forgiveness unwarranted, but it was also pointless. He didn't deserve her mercy; he deserved losing everything.

ἀπολύω translated *apolyō* [Greek]: (1) to dismiss; (2) to send; (3) to set free; (4) to go away; (5) to divorce, or divorcing; (6) to release, or released.

DIVORCE OF A DIFFERENT KIND

Paul wrote, in 1 Corinthians 3:16, that we are referred to as God's temple; it's where God lives, on the inside of us.

Carlie's temple, due to circumstances beyond her control, was under assault. She couldn't eat. She couldn't sleep. Her thoughts wouldn't slow down long enough to give her peace. The enormity of what she had been handed was like a jackhammer; a natural response was to either isolate or retaliate. Because she refused to do either, she felt vulnerable, laid bare and defenseless.

By asking Carlie to forgive, God was poised to move into the demolished areas of her life, or into her temple. In this instance, *apolyō* forgiveness became an invitation for God to fill the areas left by her husband's vacancy. By doing so, divorce could take on a new meaning. There was no ignoring the fact that Carlie was going through a painful divorce, but God was asking her to release to Him the barrage of emotions (to release them) and the physical attack upon her mind and body (to be set free), so that He could take up residence.

WHEN GOD MOVES IN

King Solomon worked tirelessly to fulfill the wishes of his father, King David, to build the Temple. We can read the story in 1 Kings 6–8. Every detail of the Temple was carried out to perfection. The glorious structure was accented with precious olive wood and the inside was covered in gold. Towering walls and ceiling planks were built of strong cypress and cedar from Lebanon. The king's labor force included 30,000 men from all over Israel, with more than 150,000 common labor and quarry workers. It took 3,300 foremen to oversee the project. The Temple was 90 feet long, 30 feet wide and 45 feet high, with additional buildings and rooms, including the inner sanctuary—the Most Holy Place.

After seven years of construction, Solomon stood and shared this compelling prayer at the site of the completed masterpiece.

Can it be that God will actually move into our neighborhood? Why, the cosmos itself isn't large enough to give you breathing room, let alone this Temple I've built. Even so, I'm bold to ask: Pay attention to these my prayers,

both intercessory and personal, O GOD, my God. Listen
to my prayers, energetic and devout, that I'm setting before you right now. Keep your eyes open to this Temple
night and day, this place of which you said, "My Name
will be honored there," and listen to the prayers that I
pray at this place. Listen from your home in heaven and
when you hear, *forgive* (1 Kings 8:27-30, *THE MESSAGE*,
emphasis added).

There is that word *apolyō*. King Solomon didn't just desire a
majestic and imposing structure. He begged God to live inside the
walls in such a way that His presence was tangible. People would
walk in and find wholeness. Those who were burdened by sin
would receive grace.

King Solomon's prayer continued as he asked God that this
Temple would be a place of justice and where relationships might
be set right. It was his hope that all nations would be attracted to
such a place as this. How could they help but be drawn to a place
where the presence of God was so richly felt?

He finally ended his prayer in 1 Kings 8:50, asking God to forgive (*apolyō*) those who had sinned and to forgive (*apolyō*) those
who had grossly rebelled. In this instance, we see forgiveness abun-
dantly embody the words "to set free," "to dismiss," "to release"
and "to divorce" (or to set aside).

Solomon could have asked for anything. In the past, God
Himself posed the question, "What do you wish to have most, my
son?" When young Solomon answered that he desired wisdom,
God poured wisdom into his life. But He didn't stop there; God
also gave Solomon riches and power (see 1 Kings 3:10-13).

Solomon could have asked God for revenge on his enemies or
on those who had unjustly pursued and harassed his family. He
had many enemies as king, not only his own, but his father's enemies as well. He could have asked God to send a scourge on those
who opposed his rule. He could have prayed that the rebellious
people be struck down when they walked into the holy Temple due
to their sin. Instead, he invited the presence of God to grace the

Temple as a place of healing, where revenge was dismissed and vengeance sent away.

Moments after his prayer ended, God spoke to King Solomon:

I have heard the prayer and plea you have made before me; I have consecrated this temple, which you have built, by putting my Name there forever. My eyes and my heart will always be there (1 Kings 9:3).

What does all this have to do with Carlie, and what does it have to do with you if you were hurt by unfaithfulness?

Carlie's sincere prayer had always been to live a life of grace. It was her deep-down desire to lead her children, alongside her husband, to know God. By God's asking her to forgive so soon, it wasn't a lack of compassion over her pain or her husband's abandonment, but a sign that God knew her well. His eyes had always seen her. His heart had always resided inside of her. God desired to mark her with His presence, putting His name there forever, no matter what her situation.

God's Job Versus Ours

As Carlie moved back into real life, the questions posed by outsiders were the hardest to answer.

What are you going to do now?

How are you going to protect yourself financially?

How could he do this and you not know?

She didn't have the answers, not yet. She was doing all that she could to get up each day and live a semi-normal life. She had vowed to herself and to her children that she would meet this challenge head-on with grace and dignity. That vow weighed heavy on her. Facebook beckoned her to blast him with one swift status update. Words spoken by her husband filtered back through mutual friends, laying the blame at her door, and they hurt so deeply she wanted to strike back with the truth.

But God was relentless with her during this season.

Forgive.

Pray blessings over him.

One night during prayer, she confessed that she would love nothing more than to smash the hood of her husband's beloved and expensive car (I love that we can be so honest with God!).

The soft, gentle "no" came quickly. It was something she'd never do, but the "no" was to her thoughts of revenge. That night, Carlie was led to the Scriptures in Matthew 6:14-15:

> If you forgive [*apolyō*] those who sin against you, your heavenly Father will forgive you. But if you refuse to forgive [*apolyō*] others, your Father will not forgive [*apolyō*] your sins (*NLT*).

As she sat in the darkness reading, she was reminded that in order to have God's mercy over her own life, she must forgive others who sin against her.

This is one of those Scriptures that challenges most of us, right? You see, in Matthew 6, Jesus had gathered His disciples around Him to teach them a new way to live. These were rough-and-tumble men who had seen something in Jesus that beckoned them to leave their jobs and families and all of their old and traditional ways. These men were in the process of transformation, seeing true miracles for the first time and setting aside ritual for relationship with the long-awaited Messiah. Jesus taught them about service, prayer and a faith that was less about memorizing the Torah and more about listening to God and responding to His voice.

Up until this time, strict rules and a system of sacrifices defined their religion. Everything in this new teaching was unsettling. One of the most unsettling was that Jesus wasn't pointing them to a complicated list of rules to carry out, but rather He was making it a heart issue.

I want you to be like my heavenly Father.

I want your decisions to reflect God's heart, rather than the ordinary or the expected.

In Carlie's case, God was whispering the same words. Her husband's secrets had turned destructive. While he initially confessed that he had been unfaithful for a matter of weeks, she discovered quickly that it had been a matter of years. This secret alone was a bombshell. It made her question everything about their relationship and even question herself. His secrets demolished his reputation. Those same secrets divided a family. They created shame and pain for all of them.

In the most private of Carlie's moments, God held out His hand to request her secrets—some of them before they even became known to her, and some so evident that they knocked her down. He asked for her thoughts of revenge that no one would ever see. He asked for her hurt. He asked for the shame that her husband had poured over her heart.

By requesting her to pray for her unfaithful husband, He was asking her to bless her enemies in the truest sense (see Matt. 5:43-44) and to forgive those who had sinned against her (see Matt. 6:12).

It is in our secrets that God desires to reside in the richest manner. It's our inner court of the temple. It's the place where thoughts are conceived that give birth to action. It's where we find solace or peace . . . or turmoil.

So Carlie stopped arguing with God. She chose to allow God to repay what should be repaid—or not. She proceeded with life. Because of her husband's choices, she had to hire a lawyer, and she made smart and prayerful decisions throughout the process. What about the emotional and spiritual battle? She placed justice—whether it was fulfilled or unfulfilled to her satisfaction—in God's hands.

FILL ME UP

This wasn't an easy decision. Forgiving her husband was not something easily done in the natural, so Carlie began to spend one hour a day in prayer. She started seeking God as never before. That one hour turned into almost two hours every night.

She read one inspirational book after another, tracking Scriptures and pouring out her heart and soul to God. She listened to worship music in her home and in her car.

None of this was an exterior act of piety, it was an intentional walk into a much deeper relationship with Christ. In the midst of her crisis, the Holy Spirit began to supernaturally heal her heart, her physical body and her soul. The more she nurtured the Presence inside of her, the less room there was for sadness, grief, anger and loss.

Weeks after her husband left, she was finally able to say the words out loud.

"I forgive him."

She knelt on the carpet and prayed blessing for her husband. There were no strings to the prayer. She didn't ask for reconciliation; her husband had made his choice clear. She wasn't asking for him to say he was sorry. She simply surrendered to God. She was offering mercy. She was forgiving the one who had sinned against her.

The next day, she woke up feeling calm. She felt God's company with her (in the inner sanctuary) for the next several hours, and that peace spanned several days. Her nerves calmed. She started to eat again. She slept more than six hours through for several nights in a row. Like a still pool of water in a raging storm, she had found peace.

Several months into the divorce process, additional secrets were revealed. She had no choice but to pray all over again on learning this painful information. Over and over again, she asked God to reside within the scarred, but sacred, walls of the temple that was her heart and thoughts.

This was key, because she needed that safe place as the divorce process played out. It was painful to communicate through a lawyer after nearly 30 years of marriage. It was hard to watch the man she married choose to be with another person. It was hard to experience the nitty-gritty of dividing assets and seeing your life on white paper in neat columns. The numbers could never add up to what they had lost, because the loss had little to do with money.

She continued to have to make difficult decisions. She continued to have to deal with hard truths. But she was never alone, because God's peace had made its home inside of her.

An Ongoing Process

One year later, Carlie continues to *apolyō* forgive. She prays that her ex-husband will one day reconnect with his Savior. She prays for godly friends who will help lead him back to Christ. She prays that his relationship with their children can ultimately be healed and that their future grandchildren will one day be a part of his life.

She has no preconceived ideas about what that might look like. She has moved on with her life. Forgiving has allowed her to look back and treasure the good times with her entire family, the early years of their marriage and the gifts she received in the form of her son and daughter.

She revels in her everyday blessings, even in the challenges as a newly single woman of faith. She is thankful for strong friendships and for extended family, but most of all, for her relationship with her God.

Healing and forgiving is an ongoing process. As Carlie has discovered, there's always opportunity for additional hurt, but she has chosen to celebrate the milestones rather than the obstacles.

What Are Those Milestones?

David Seamands, in his book *Healing for Damaged Emotions,* offers the following tests for forgiveness:

1. Can you thank God for the lessons learned in pain?
2. Can you talk about the event without anger or feelings of revenge?
3. Have you accepted your part of the blame for what happened?
4. Can you revisit the scene without a negative reaction?[2]

The goal of questions such as these is to help you honestly assess how far you've come and where to go next. These are hard questions to ask because they focus on you, rather than on the offender. But isn't that the point?

The lessons you learn through unfaithfulness may be "never trust anyone" or "something must be wrong with me" or "my life is forever ruined." This thinking can keep you from discovering what life might hold beyond the threshold of unfaithfulness. But it's also a time to acknowledge the lessons you've learned that moved you past unforgiveness into wholeness, such as, "I can do all things through Christ who strengthens me" (Phil. 4:13, *NKJV*) or, "Greater is He who is in [me] than he who is in the world" (1 John 4:4, *NASB*).

The second question that David Seamands asks is crucial.

The reason I pursued forgiveness in my own life is that I didn't want my children to have a bitter, angry woman for a mother. Due to my childhood, I had reason to be angry, but when I looked at my children I had more incentive to be whole and joy-filled. At some point, we offer up and release those feelings, no matter how good or justified they make us feel. It doesn't mean that you won't encounter those feelings or emotions again, but they no longer hold you hostage.

When I consider the past, it's a small part of my identity. It shaped me, but it doesn't define me. It is a chapter in the book of my life; but if you read the back cover copy you will find so much more than my past in that description. I'm a mom. I'm a wife. I am a gramma (one of my favorite parts). I hike. I love rafting. I'm not an early morning person. I think cheesecake is always worth the calories. Flower gardens and springtime always make me happy. I love roller coasters. I zip-lined on my last birthday, and one day I hope to jump out of a plane. All of these elements are snippets of my identity.

When we begin to see ourselves through a larger lens, we revisit the past and point out with precision the parts we wish hadn't happened, as well as what has taken place since then. We also become scholars of the past, learning what we want to carry forward and what we wish to do differently. When we speak of the past, we give it its proper place. It's not ignored, but it doesn't receive a greater share than it deserves.

Often, as I sit with women who feel stuck or who are still angry and resentful, I discover that they remain mired as they revisit the actions of others, living as though completely defined by one person or a series of events, some of them years and years in the past. This gives that event or that person far more power than deserved.

That leads to the third and perhaps most difficult question: What is your part in this? This is the question that stumped some of the women who came alongside as I wrote this book. They said things like this:

Come on, Suzie. I don't see how blaming myself is an option here.

How could anyone ask this, especially when someone has been unfaithful? I didn't do anything wrong. This isn't a fair question.

Believe me, I understand how hard it is to ask this question. Perhaps the problem is with the word "blame." It's such a strong word. But let's take a step back to look at the picture as a whole so that we can gain insight. None of us, even in the strongest of relationships, is stuck in a no-growth pattern. In Carlie's case, she says that her belief that she can fix anything or do anything if she puts her mind to it is both a strength and weakness. Her husband's leaving shattered that belief.

She couldn't fix him. She couldn't fix them. Discovering that you can't make a person love you more or treat you the way they should was a powerful insight for her. This insight allows her to freely admit that she is worth loving for who she is. This knowledge will benefit a future relationship when she is ready, but it also frees her today.

Perhaps your answer to that question is "I did everything that I could." That alone is freeing. It offers permission to move forward without regret or second-guessing.

The last question David Seamands suggests is a milestone question for certain: *Can you revisit the scene without a negative reaction?* We instinctively associate sights, sounds, smell and other senses to a person or moment in time. I can't help but be swept into nostalgia when I smell the scent of a smoking pipe. The sweet, woodsy scent of a certain tobacco reminds me of my dad. Certain songs take me to the skating rink in Tulsa, Oklahoma, where I flew around the rink, my long brown hair flying behind me at the age of 13, hoping Barry (the cutest guy in school) was watching.

Over time, as you heal, places and people are put into perspective. Perhaps it is too fresh at this point, but there comes a time when you walk past that place or you see that person and you view him or her through eyes of wholeness. You may feel sadness, but you don't feel bound. You can walk away without fingers of the past trying to draw you back into emotions and feelings already restored. There is no room or place or person powerful enough to cloud the fact that while you once were affected, you no longer live (abide) there.

Carlie is on a new path. She says, "I'm discovering God's will for my life. I believe that I will have companionship again. Divorce is an ugly thing, but it doesn't define me. An unwanted divorce is what happened to me. My relationship with my heavenly Father defines me; the way I treat and love others defines me; my sense of humor, my sensitive heart, my love of life, my family and friends and my spirit for adventure define me, . . . but not divorce."

Today, unexpected joy surprises Carlie, just as tears once did.

When Your Temple Is in Ruins

You are God's temple, his daughter, and He lives in you. You may feel that you are in ruins today, but His presence and unfailing faithfulness is able to rebuild the hope and trust that has been battered or even shattered. Perhaps, like Carlie, you've sensed God asking you to forgive. Maybe He's asked you to hand Him your secrets. What is He saying to you?

You are questioning your worth, daughter. Define yourself by My love instead.

You are angry, daughter. I understand, but let Me take that burden.

Your thoughts of revenge aren't in My plan for you. Let Me have them so you can devote time and energy to things of value.

Looking back to day three, when God initially asked Carlie to forgive, she believes that He didn't really expect her to be able to forgive so soon. He was simply planting a seed of forgiveness, because the sooner she could allow that to take root in her heart, the sooner she would begin healing.

IF YOU ARE TRYING TO WORK IT OUT

Perhaps you chose to remain in your marriage and are working things out. It's not smooth sailing yet, but you and your spouse have hope that it will.

You may question why it's so hard to forgive even in the face of repentance. It is because unfaithfulness shakes the foundation of trust. Tammy Maltby, in *The God Who Sees You*, takes that struggle even deeper. She says that trauma changes the fabric of normal. She goes on to say:

> I'm convinced that it's not the trauma itself that does the most damage in our lives. It's the false conclusions that we draw about God that leave the biggest scars. It's the mistaken belief that God doesn't care or isn't in control or that He actually sets out to hurt us. And believing such a thing is too painful. It feels safer to believe that God doesn't see us—or that He doesn't even exist.[3]

If your trust has been betrayed, the thought of forgiving might make you feel vulnerable, not just with your spouse but with God. You might think that it's impossible to forgive. And you are right on every count. It does make you vulnerable; but don't confuse vulnerability with weakness. To be vulnerable simply means that you choose not to live a sheltered, fenced-in life that keeps you hemmed in.

Give yourself permission to be honest with your heavenly Father, but with the understanding that there is nothing in Scripture that condones unfaithfulness. It's not in God's plan or His character. And if this same God grieves over the fallen sparrow (see

Matt. 10:29), then He grieves over your broken relationship. He is big enough to handle your honesty while leading you to a new level of spiritual joy and intimacy and even tender vulnerability in your relationship with Him.

At this moment, it may seem impossible to forgive on your own, but are you willing? That's the only question you need to answer.

If that's where you are today, and the answer is yes, I am willing, then that's faith! You have just admitted what you cannot do on your own, and you have surrendered to what God wants to do in and for you as you offer up a willing heart. That's one of the strongest, most faith-filled, steps a person can take!

JUST YOU AND GOD

1. Carlie spent time daily reading Scripture and listening to worship music. How are you currently filling the empty places left by unfaithfulness? What do you feel God nudging you to do differently?

2. *Apolyō* forgiveness means to dismiss, to set free or to go away. What do you desire to go away or dismiss or set free? (If you struggle to find the words, simply write Matt. 6:9-13.)

3. Do you believe that God is aware of the value of your forgiveness? If so, how does this impact your decision to forgive?

_____

_____

_____

_____

_____

4. Ask the questions posed in this chapter by David Seamands in his book *Healing for Damaged Emotions* and honestly answer them here. Make a note to return to these questions one week from now, one month from now and one year from now. Celebrate every milestone of healing found in your responses.

_____

_____

_____

_____

_____

5. You are God's temple. He lives in you. Take a spiritual flashlight and invite God to look in every room with you. What do you see? What is God asking you to hurl away, dismiss or set free today?

_____

_____

_____

_____

_____

_____

Apolyō Principle

God's presence comes in and takes residence.

To *Apolyō* Forgive

Intentionally invite God into the demolished areas of
your mind, body and spirit.

Prayer

*God, You are faithful always. I want to be a temple filled with
Your presence. Let healing begin! I offer up my secrets. I let go of
unhealthful lessons learned. You and Your plans for me are my
strong foundation. Let's continue to grow . . . together.*

Notes

1. Not her real name.
2. David A. Seamands, *Healing for Damaged Emotions* (Colorado Springs, CO: David C. Cook, 1991).
3. Tammy Maltby and Anne Christian Buchanan, *The God Who Sees You: Look to Him When You Feel Discouraged, Forgotten, or Invisible* (Colorado Springs, CO: David C. Cook, 2012), chapter 6.

4

You Move Past What You Cannot Change

Forgiveness is not forgetting; it is simply denying your pain the right to control your life.

Corallie Buchanan, *Watch Out! Godly Women on the Loose*

Injustice is defined as an act that is unmerited, unfair or outright wrong.

Joe and Barbie understand that definition; you see, they look into the face of it every single day. Their daughter, Felicia, was born after several years of trying to conceive. When she finally arrived, they were overjoyed. When it was time for Barbie to go back to work, they agonized over the choice of childcare. After weeks of searching, they finally chose a friend to watch over their daughter, confident that Felicia would be loved and in a safe environment while Barbie worked part-time.

One day, the sitter called and begged Barbie to come quickly. When Barbie walked through the door, Felicia was unresponsive. Joe had arrived and they grabbed their baby and jumped in the car and sped to a nearby doctor's office. Joe drove while Barbie administered CPR. Joe veered into the parking lot and they rushed through the door as Barbie continued to breathe life into her daughter.

Their baby was taken by Life Flight to a trauma hospital. It was there that the parents were told their daughter's condition was grave. That night a priest came to pray at her bedside while they stood helplessly nearby.

In the crush of the emergency, neither parent had considered that their baby's condition might be due to abuse. But as the police questioned the sitter, she tearfully confessed that Felicia was crying and wouldn't stop. She had lost her temper and shook the baby until she was quiet. While Joe and Barbie sat at their daughter's side in the hospital, the sitter was arraigned.

Later that week, physicians informed the parents that their little girl had been shaken so badly that she would never communicate. She was blind and in a vegetative state. The prognosis was dire; doctors could not see her living beyond the age of five years old.

When the couple finally brought their baby home, Barbie went into protective mode. She didn't let anyone touch Felicia. She didn't leave the house. She sat with her daughter in her arms and wept, all the while thinking of ways to punish the offender, hoping that one day the sitter would experience the same pain she felt. Meanwhile, Joe plunged into his work. He often daydreamed and pictured the sitter at a busy intersection, wondering what it would be like to broadside the woman who hurt his daughter.

In the months after their daughter was hurt, their marriage suffered. They were in so much pain that they pulled away from each other, feeling isolated and alone in their little family of three.

One day, a family member took Joe aside. "Have you thought about forgiving her?" he asked.

Initially, the question made Joe angry; but as he considered the last several months, he confessed that his anger had not eased his pain. The greatest source of his frustration, beyond his daughter's injuries, was the injustice of it all. The sitter had received a suspended 10-year sentence with no jail time. She walked the streets free while his daughter had received a life sentence of disability.

As they talked, he confessed that the anger and what-ifs were a burden that weighed him down, and thoughts of revenge consumed him.

Joe didn't know that several days earlier another family member had prayed with Barbie, and she had opened her heart just wide enough to let Christ in. It just wasn't something she felt she could share with her husband . . . not yet.

Later that night, the couple sat down and talked for the first time since their daughter was hurt. Joe confessed that while he didn't know how or why, he wanted to forgive. Barbie was reluctant. How was that even possible?

They sat together for hours and discussed how the incident and associated emotions had affected their marriage and each other. They both knew that forgiving wouldn't change what happened, but they were exhausted by the burden they carried.

Joe made a phone call and asked if he and Barbie could meet with the sitter, and he was surprised when she accepted. The meeting was far from comfortable. The sitter sat on the couch, leery, with her arms crossed. Her husband seemed relieved, but silent. It was awkward at best. After a short time, Barbie and Joe left without any tangible resolution. They talked in the car, acknowledging that nothing short of a miracle could change Felicia's condition, but they both felt that somehow they had taken the right step.

NOT FAIR!

Now, this is where I struggled. As I listened to Joe and Barbie, I was in awe of the depth of their sincere faith and grace; but as a mother, I had trouble grasping the measure of forgiveness they had given. If you were to ask 100,000 parents if the sitter who shook Felicia deserved forgiveness, the answer would be absolutely not.

And she didn't.

Barbie and Joe offered something of great value to someone who didn't deserve it, didn't want it and didn't know how to receive it properly.

But they chose to do it anyway.

This began a series of determined choices for this couple. They lived in the same small city as the woman who harmed their child and would run into each other by accident. One day, Joe crossed the street and spoke to her. Barbie stood quietly by. As her husband talked with the woman, Barbie silently offered her resentment and anger to the Lord, placing her hurt in hands bigger than her own. She kept her focus on her heavenly Father, asking Him to help her in the moment, and somehow He did.

In the book *An Invitation to Healing*, Lynda Elliott wrote about a terrible struggle she had with a neighbor when she was in her twenties. "For months, I replayed the hurtful scene in my mind," she wrote, "talking about it often with a friend. As I expressed my feelings over and over, my pain became deeper and more invasive. It was becoming a part of me."[1]

One day, as Lynda relived the scene again, her friend asked, "Do you know we become like the people we think about most?" Lynda reveals that she had a choice to make. She wrote, "If I chose to behold Jesus, to focus on Him, I could be transformed into His image. Likewise, if I continued to behold the image of my neighbor, I could be transformed into her image. In fact, that was already happening."[2]

Barbie and Joe were handed an unfair, unjust twist of life. They didn't do anything other than try to be good parents. They were new Christians; but as Barbie and Joe searched out Scripture, they chose to grow into the image of Christ and reflect Him in the midst of injustice, even without a clear understanding of what that looked like or what it meant.

> **χαρίζομαι** translated *charizomai* [Greek]: (1) to frankly forgive; (2) to give graciously; (3) pardon; (4) give freely; (5) bestow.

Their battle was so much more than a hurtful neighbor or a mother-in-law that says all the wrong things. And this injustice would never go away. Their daughter needed 24/7 care, and there was no end in sight. They love her and nurture her, many times exhausted, with the knowledge that she will never grow into the woman she would have otherwise.

Today, Felicia is in her late twenties. She is known throughout our church as the angel who sings with the choir. She is still blind. She does not communicate with words, but she smiles and she launches into her own special melody in praise and worship.

The injustice of one woman's bad mood bringing permanent damage to their child has caused Joe and Barbie to deal with the aftermath of injustice on a daily basis. They continue to forgive; and when it's exhausting, they say that they kneel and pray together instead of pushing away from each other. They choose forgiveness over bitterness and regret; and forgiveness continues to change something on the inside of this couple. The unjust act that took place with beautiful Felicia did not, could not, go away; but somehow this couple was able to live again and continue to live free.

WHEN FORGIVENESS IS UNDERSERVED

Charizomai forgiveness is restorative forgiveness. It requires that Jesus walk beside us as we make intentional choices to forgive; but more so, it means to unload the weight of a thousand pounds off of our minds and hearts.

Charizomai forgiveness is from the heart and is given without restraint, with or without merit. It is exactly the kind of mercy Paul reflected in his speech and conduct when unfairly handed over to the religious authorities in Jerusalem, and later in Rome when surrounded by a hostile crowd who were once his neighbors and kinsmen. We see this word again when Paul is on a ship, still a prisoner, on his way to stand before Caesar, and he's caught in the middle of a storm so violent that the sun was blackened for days and days.

When Saul (he was later renamed Paul) became a Christian, he knew that persecution would be his fate, but did he know how extensive the injustice might be? Paul was beaten nearly to death, imprisoned unfairly and held for over two years without a trial. He was so discouraged at one point that God whispered in his ear, "Take courage!" (Acts 23:11). You know that if God Himself comes to you in the middle of the night, you are hurting!

Now Paul is finally on his way to Rome to defend himself when he's trapped in a storm so destructive that the crew is tossing provisions overboard for a chance to survive. In that moment, Paul offered hope to the men who were holding him captive, saying, "Last night an angel of the God to whom I belong and whom I serve stood beside me and said, 'Do not be afraid, Paul. You must stand trial before Caesar; and God has graciously given [*charizomai*] you the lives of all who sail with you.' So keep up your courage, men, for I have faith in God that it will happen just as he told me. Nevertheless, we must run aground on some island" (Acts 27:23-26).

His own fate was in question, and Paul owed these men nothing. He could have left them with their fear. He could have watched as they pitched their own bodies overboard into the frothing waves rather than ram into the reef, but he gave them something they didn't deserve instead.

He didn't do it out of his own strength. It came out of an encounter with God the night before—one that was so intimate that Paul reminded them that he *belonged* to God. Even in that harsh environment, surrounded by wind and slashing rain, in shackles and uncertainty, Paul knew that he was not alone.

WHY DO WE TRY TO FORGIVE ON OUR OWN?

In Luke 7, Jesus was in a crowd of people who were very sick. He was "healing many [people] of sicknesses and distressing bodily plagues and evil spirits, and to many who were blind He gave [a free, gracious, joy-giving gift of] sight" (Luke 7:21 *AMP*). In this scene, the crowd presses in because nothing else has worked. Doctors can't fix them. They are sick and tired of being sick and tired.

I nearly danced with joy when I discovered that the root word for "gave" in this passage is *charizomai*. When we live a forgiving lifestyle, we give; but we also receive!

There were many moments when Barbie and Joe struggled: in the middle of the night, when Felicia cried for hours, and they were fatigued; during the trial when they were bombarded with emotions as the judgment was handed down and it didn't fit the crime. They struggled as their daughter experienced frightening seizures. Each time, they acknowledged their feelings and were truthful with each other and with God, but they placed judgment and retribution in God's lap. They also asked Him to help them in their pain.

They *charizomai* forgave, but also *charizomai* received.

Just as forgiveness is a conscious decision, so is the resolve to handle this on our own. The rationale is that the offender must be punished. We must take matters into our own hands. Perhaps forgiving seems like such a remote possibility that you plow through each day, hoping tomorrow will be better. You grit your teeth and try to manhandle your way through it.

It's frustrating when you just keep feeling the same old feelings.

But while you are trying to work it out on your own, how does it affect your family? What is the cost in your relationships? What does it cost your health? Your emotional wellbeing? You belong to God. He sees you. What happened to you matters to God because you matter to Him.

You don't have to do this alone.

Where do you begin as you work together with God to *charizomai* forgive?

RECOGNIZE THE INJUSTICE

Lewis Smedes, in his book *Forgive and Forget*, wrote, "When we forgive evil we do not excuse it, we do not tolerate it, we do not smother it."[2] Forgiving doesn't mean that you pretend it didn't happen. Our memories are intertwined with our emotions and our thought processes. So are the negative emotions that make it difficult to let go. Some people assume that forgiving means that you ignore what took place, or you put on a good face and bury it so that you can move on. After all, you can't change it, so why dwell on it?

Neither of these options is healthful.

I visited with a woman after a conference who confessed that her father molested her as a child. She recalled passing her mom on the stairs one day. They both stopped and stared at each other. Neither said a word, but it was as if an entire conversation took place in seconds. She realized that her mother knew and that the adults in her life would either harm her or look the other way.

When she ended the story, she fidgeted with her tissue. She brushed away tears and then with a bright smile that didn't reach her eyes, she said, "It's okay now. Sorry I burdened you with that."

All I could think at that moment was, *You're trying to make me feel better?*

I assured her that she didn't have to offer a happy twist on her story and that what happened was unjust. Her father never should have molested his own daughter. Her mother should have rescued her.

Not only is it okay to tell the truth about what took place, it's necessary. And yet, we don't often do that, perhaps out of fear that we'll be misunderstood or that we'll be seen as a victim rather than a beautiful, strong woman.

Maybe we don't want to be *that* person who wraps her identity around the past or tells the same stories one after the other. David wrote, speaking of God, in Psalm 51:6, "Behold, You desire truth in the inmost being, and in the hidden part You will make me know wisdom" (*NASB*) When we are honest with ourselves, we stop pushing down those feelings, and those emotions can be addressed.

God, who knows you best, desires you to live in the light; and truth is the light switch. Listen, there is a vast difference between living perennially wounded and simply being honest about what took place.

When you tell the truth, you leave the door wide open for healing.

The woman I met at the conference had never given herself permission to grieve or to speak honestly about how her father's abuse and her mother's failure to rescue her had affected her. It was a hush-hush secret in her family. Recognizing the injustice was the first step she could take toward healing.

DON'T TAKE JUSTICE IN YOUR OWN HANDS

Once you speak the truth, you place justice in God's hands. But let's be honest, this goes against how we feel. This is not to say that we don't pursue legal ramifications for those who break the law, or that we fail to implement change or boundaries where it is vitally needed; but we do allow God in His provident wisdom to be the ultimate judge.

Paul wrote, "Do not take revenge, my dear friends, but leave room for God's wrath, for it is written: 'It is mine to avenge; I will repay,' says the Lord" (Rom. 12:19). The courts may or may not offer the sentence you believe is sufficient, but at some point the price you have paid is high enough if you continue to punish the person in your heart.

Joe and Barbie are close friends, and I have known them for more than 25 years. Felicia was hurt before we met. When Joe shared how he fantasized about broadsiding his daughter's offender, I could picture the busy intersection he described, but I couldn't place Joe behind the wheel. I could see him teasing Joie and Robin, his younger daughters. I could picture him on a rooftop in an African village with a hammer in his hand, helping put a roof on a steel-beam church. I could imagine him kissing Barbie on the cheek or teasing her, because I had seen it a hundred times before.

But harming another person? No.

Joe vividly remembers the temptation to take justice in his own hands. The system failed his daughter. The offender never served a day in jail. Yet, Joe and Barbie are the ones who say they are free.

David A. Stoop, in his book *Forgiving the Unforgivable*, wrote:

> Our forgiving the other person does not in any way benefit or let him or her off the hook. It allows us to cancel the debt they owe us, which in all probability they cannot pay anyway. We are the ones who are freed—from the expectation of restitution for the wrongs done to us.[3]

WHAT IF I'M NOT READY?

In the beginning pages of this book, I shared that God meets us where we are. He kneels in the dust beside the broken woman. He goes out of His way to help the lame man stand to his feet. He traveled across tumultuous waters and stood in the gate of a cemetery to loose the chains of a man bound by torment. Setting people free is the very reason He came to earth.

When we start the process of *charizomai* forgiving, we simply ask God to meet us right where we are, whether that is day one of the injustice or, as in Barbie and Joe's case, day 10,220 and counting; whether we are so angry we struggle to sleep at night because we can't think of anything else; or we've taken huge strides but are tired of doing it through our own strength.

It's also asking Him to fill the void. As you take steps to forgive, there will be an empty place where anger used to live. Robert D. Enright, in his book *Forgiveness Is a Choice*, wrote:

> I believe when the resentment leaves, that place should not be left void, but instead can be filled with positive feelings. Although this may seem impossible we have found in our research that in some of the hardest cases people were able to achieve full forgiveness.[4]

Enright's studies discovered that positive feelings came as people helped others, as they supported those harmed in the same way or as they joined to prevent it from recurring. There are thousands of organizations that have emerged as a result of turning a negative into a positive, and these are helpful and needed.

While helping others is a powerful response to injustice, what do you do when the task is complete or you are alone without the busyness? That's when *charizomai* forgiveness is invaluable, because this type of forgiveness is a joint effort. In almost every Scripture where we are encouraged to *charizomai* forgive, we are reminded of where we find that source. It's a supernatural reserve graciously given to us from which we can scoop what we need to give to others.

It's you and God in tandem.

This is the key to *charizomai* forgiveness. This is where we fall short when we say to people, "Just forgive." Perhaps you feel that you've been asked to do this on your own, to somehow scrape up the willpower necessary to forgive someone who doesn't deserve it. Maybe it feels as if a pastor or a friend or caring Christians have said that the grave injustice you or your loved one faced is equivalent to the irk felt toward a neighbor who is quarrelsome and gossipy. And that just doesn't make sense.

You are right. You aren't required to forgive by willpower alone. It's impossible; and when others ask you to do this, they place a heavier burden on you than you already carry. It's not the same offense, and it requires more than you can do by yourself. *Charizomai* forgiveness takes into consideration that "everything else is worthless when compared with the infinite value of knowing Christ Jesus" (Phil. 3:8, *NLT*).

What does that mean to you? Because you are beloved of Christ, He offers what you need. There is value in being a child of God. You can stop striving to feel what you cannot feel.

Just let it go, they say.

You reply, "God is with me right where I'm at. I know He is healing me, and I know that one day, with His help, I'll forgive. I look forward to that day."

With *charizomai* forgiveness, you affirm that what happened matters greatly to God, so much that there is an open invitation from God to help you do what you cannot possibly do without His intervention.

Over time, with you and God in tandem, He takes that burden, which Joe described as a "wall of bricks sitting on my shoulders," and it falls away so that you can breathe again.

WHAT PAUL WANTED US TO KNOW

The book of Romans was written in the bleakest and most unjust period of Paul's life. This changes the way we read Scriptures such as these:

> And we know that in all things God works for the good of those who love him, who have been called according to his purpose (Rom. 8:28).

> What, then, shall we say in response to these things? If God is for us, who can be against us? (Rom. 8:31).

Who shall separate us from the love of Christ? Shall trouble or hardship or persecution or famine or nakedness or danger or sword? (Rom. 8:35).

No, in all these things we are more than conquerors through him who loved us. For I am convinced that neither death nor life, neither angels nor demons, neither the present nor the future, nor any powers, neither height nor depth, nor anything else in all creation, will be able to separate us from the love of God that is in Christ Jesus our Lord (Rom. 8:37-39).

Though injustice pressed in on every side, Paul found a deeper source as a child of God. Read these passages from Romans one more time. Put Paul in that jail cell or on that twisting, thrashing ship. See his questions.

God, Have You Forgotten Me?

Empathize with Paul's desire to travel to churches, to share the gospel, to come alongside disciples, to travel with the message God had burned on his heart. His life had been changed on the road to Damascus. He was the same man who once plunged into homes with zeal and dragged out people to their death in a fury to wipe out the cause of Christianity. But once he encountered Christ, that same personality and zeal was focused on telling others how wrong he had been and how right it was to love and know Jesus Christ. How bridled he must have felt.

Imagine old friends and neighbors outside plotting his death because he dared to call himself a Christian.

How is it possible in light of these emotions and experiences that he wrote such intimate words with such conviction? He was reminded of the forgiveness he had been graciously given by God "who did not spare his own Son, but gave him up for us all—how will he not also, along with him, graciously give us all things?" (Rom. 8:32). And out of that deep well, he found hope, which not only sustained him, but helped him pen words that reached generations later into our hearts.

Suzie, I'm Not Paul

I disagree. We are all Paul. We are all ordinary individuals who follow an extraordinary God. Joe is a mill worker and a part-time maintenance employee at his church. Barbie is an administrative assistant. They are rarely in the spotlight, and they don't have a public platform. They don't have a blog. Their life story will never be flashed across the pages of the *New York Times*. They allowed me to share this story because they wanted others who are struck by injustice to know that when a person *charizomai* forgives, it doesn't alter the events of the past, but it does allow you to find joy again.

JUST YOU AND GOD

1. Have you acknowledged the injustice you have faced? Write it down. Speak the truth.

   _____

   _____

   _____

   _____

2. Explain why you are ready to stop the cycle of punishment of your offender in your heart and thoughts.

   _____

   _____

   _____

   _____

3. As you read Barbie and Joe's story, did you identify with them? How does their story help you as you forgive?

   _____

   _____

   _____

4. In 2 Corinthians 2:10-11, *charizomai* forgiveness is used five times. Paul advises us to forgive so that the enemy's schemes are revealed and put to rest. How does forgiving (with God's help) release you from that scheme?

_____

_____

_____

_____

_____

5. Read Romans 8:26-27. In Rome, Paul faced injustice on every side. He most likely felt alone. What encouragement do you find in these Scriptures penned by Paul?

_____

_____

_____

_____

_____

6. In this chapter, I state that "we are all Paul." What does that mean to you personally?

_____

_____

_____

_____

_____

CHARIZOMAI PRINCIPLE

To consciously give to another what they cannot give themselves, as you have received graciously from God.

TO CHARIZOMAI FORGIVE

Stop trying to do it by yourself.

PRAYER

My Savior, You were unjustly treated. I am grateful that You do not ignore how hurt I am or how impossible it would be to forgive on my own. Every day You extend mercy to me. Pour that mercy overflowing into my heart and into my thoughts, and begin to do what I cannot.

Notes

1. Lynda Elliott, *An Invitation to Healing: Let God Touch Your Mind Body and Spirit* (Grand Rapids, MI: Chosen Books, 2001).
2. Ibid.
3. Lewis Smedes, *Forgive and Forget: Healing the Hurts We Don't Deserve* (New York: Pocket Books, 1990), p. 107.
4. David A. Stoop, *Forgiving the Unforgivable* (Ventura, CA: Regal Books, 2005), p. 35.
5. Robert D. Enright, "Forgiveness Is a Choice: A Step-by-Step Process for Resolving Anger and Restoring Hope" (Washington DC: *American Psychological Association* (APA), May 2001), p. 36.

5

You Receive Your New Identity

No longer will they call you Deserted, or name your land
Desolate. But you will be called Hephzibah, and your land Beulah;
for the LORD will take delight in you.

Isaiah 62:4

As Candy parked her bike at school, a mother came up to her and said, "Why are your clothes dirty?"

Candy looked down at the dried dirt on her jeans.

"You always come to school dirty," the woman said.

Candy had picked up the jeans that morning from her bedroom floor. Her mother had started abusing drugs and alcohol when her father was in the process of leaving, and it only spiraled after he left. Bills piled up. There were times when Candy arrived at school hungry, her hair uncombed and her teeth not brushed. As a second grader, she was proud of making it to school by herself. But the woman's words reduced her pride to shame. School was hard. Candy spent many recesses with the teacher and a lot of her school hours in the nurse's office. It seemed that the children at school wanted nothing to do with her.

One day, a girl stopped her as Candy was riding by on her bike, and they played. The girl was well liked in school by teachers and students. Her father was a small-business owner and her mother a teacher. Over the next few weeks they played together several times, and somehow there was an unspoken understanding that they were friends, but only in private. Their friendship was to be kept from the girl's *real* friends.

One day as they played, the girl's mother drove by slowly and then stopped. The strong words she spoke to her daughter carried to Candy in the wind. The girl returned and explained that she had to leave, and they drove away. But her excuse did not wipe away the hurt from the words Candy had overheard.

A few weeks later, Candy rode her bike past her old friend's house and saw her playing outside. She needed to go to the bathroom, and home was a distance away, so she asked if she could use her friend's bathroom. The girl went inside, and after several moments she came out and hung her head. "My mother is cleaning," she said. "You can't come in."

During her desperate ride home the little girl embraced shame all over again as her identity.

After that, she learned to be alone. She sat in the dust of the front yard to escape harsh words that came from inside, words like, "Go play on the Interstate" or "I brought home the wrong child from the hospital" or "I'm going to kill myself."

The unspoken message was to leave people alone.

When Candy was almost 13, her mother moved to subsidized housing. Candy had two younger siblings, and she often was asked to skip school to watch the two- and three-year-old. Her mother wouldn't come home for days in a row. Candy often felt trapped and fearful because there wasn't enough to eat. Her mother would return unexpectedly only to leave again.

One day, a social services lady came by.

"Is your mother home?" she asked. "Do you have food in the house?"

Candy lied. Her mother had informed her that social services would separate her from her siblings and send them to different homes; and if that happened it would be her fault. So Candy explained how her mother washed her clothes, cleaned the apartment and came home all the time. She painted a picture of the mom she wished she had, and the social worker went away.

As a teen, she went to work at a fast-food restaurant. One day a girl came up to her. "My mom says we are supposed to be friends," she said. For the next year, Candy went to church with her new acquaintance. The awkward beginning turned into a real friendship; and one day, as they sat together in church, the words that had been spoken from the pulpit for months suddenly felt like they were for her.

They were words that said she was lovely. Worthy. Clean.

> אישנ [Hebrew] translated *nasa* (1) raiser; (2) lifted up; (3) carried; (4) burden-bearer; (5) armor bearer; (6) exultation.

DEFINED BY SHAME VERSUS DESIRED BY GOD

Shame is a heavy burden. It's born of secrets that are a reminder that you and your circumstances are different from others' and are so shameful that you can't speak of them. When you do, you take a chance that people might not know what to say. The last thing you want is to be perceived with pity, or to cast your burden upon the shoulders of the listener. So you bear it alone.

Isaiah 43:18-19 became reality for Candy. "Forget about what's happened; don't keep going over old history. Be alert, be present. I'm about to do something brand-new. It's bursting out! Don't you see it?" (*THE MESSAGE*).

Becoming new meant that the words of others and her past couldn't define her anymore. Profound, right? But challenging, nevertheless.

After college, she sat with friends over lunch as they chatted about old friends back home. The conversation moved to someone Candy didn't know. They talked about the person's new lifestyle, new house, new stuff until one girl commented, "She may think she's better, but she's still trash. Look at where she came from." Silence reigned. Eyes turned to Candy as they realized their mistake. Candy froze.

Is that how they see me too?

"Sorry, Candy," another girl said.

This presented a choice. Candy could embrace shame or choose to define herself through Scripture. It wasn't the first time, nor would it be the last to make that choice. When you've been marked by ugly words spoken again and again, leaving behind that mirror image of yourself is not easy.

John MacArthur, in his book *The Freedom and Power of Forgiveness*, wrote, "Ultimately a conscious, deliberate, willful choice is the only thing that can free a heart from the bondage of such emotions."[1]

But how do you make that choice?

Nasa forgiveness means to raise up, to lift or to exalt. It also carries a secondary meaning to be a burden-bearer or armor bearer—one who steps in to carry a heavy load or to stand in the way of arrows that fly toward an unprotected heart. In the Old Testament, we find these loyal servants walking two steps ahead and two steps behind those they had sworn to protect, their arms laden with weapons that might be needed in battle.

The word *nasa* is found only in the Old Testament and is an underlying theme in stories of bravery as a hero defeats his foe or as someone steps up to defend another. It's also found in Scripture passages such as 1 Chronicles 15:26, where the word *nasa* reveals the ark being lifted and carried because of its preciousness to God.

Each of these meanings translates powerfully to the person who has experienced shame and desires to forgive.

Nasa forgiveness allows you to hand your secrets and shame to Someone who takes them willingly simply because you are precious to Him. It elevates you to a place of worth already established in God's viewpoint—not because of where you live or what you look like, or what you've accomplished, or because or in spite of your past, but because your name is etched on the palm of God's hand (see Isa. 49:16).

SHAME AND FORGIVENESS CANNOT COEXIST

Many of us can identify with Candy. Words were thoughtlessly aimed our way by peers or adults, or we were shamed by the person who should have kept us out of harm's way.

In the Old Testament, the armor bearer rose up as a human shield for someone of great importance. Armor bearers were servants, but they were also loyal companions. Abimelek (see Judg. 9:54), Saul (see 1 Sam. 16:21) and Jonathan (see 1 Sam. 14:6-17) were all served by armor bearers. If an enemy stalked his prey to steal, kill or shame him, the enemy was met with a wall of resistance because of the armor bearers. Strong and mighty men carrying weapons of warfare hemmed in the one they protected. If the enemy was going to take out his prey, he must first get through the armor bearers. Armor bearers were also responsible for finishing the job. After enemy soldiers were wounded with javelins or bows and arrows, armor bearers made sure they met with a swift death.

Armor-bearers didn't keep their master out of harm's way; they walked with him through it.

Therefore, when *nasa* forgiveness encounters shame, it lifts that forgiver up and over shame to the place of value already held by God. The burden is shifted to God's broad shoulders, and He is now free to complete the "good work began in you" (see Phil. 1:6).

In Candy's case, she had learned some ill-fitting lessons:

- Stay low.
- Don't talk, because what you have to say isn't worth hearing.
- Your secrets are your burden to bear.
- You must not be worth being loved.

These lessons can cause a person to try to fill those gaps, sometimes with people, sometimes with a desire for attention or even the complete opposite as he or she tries to stay well out of the limelight. It can also cause confusion over one's true identity.

Christian speaker Connie Davis Johnson says that shame places a pencil in our hands:

We give that pencil to others and we say, "tell us who we are." If they write words that hurt, we embrace that as our story. If they say we are pretty, we open up our heart because it's what we long to hear. Even if they are a good person, if they hold the pencil and there is a bad day, we question the words they wrote the day before. Sometimes, whether in a marriage or a relationship, we depend upon that pencil from day to day, and if it fails to give us what we need, we take the pencil away and give it to another, hoping they'll write the words we wish to hear. Affairs and unhealthy relationships take place as we carry that pencil from one person to the next, hoping to erase the shame we bear, because no one person should be responsible to write our story. God is the only one who can truly hold the pencil. Regardless of our past, or what others say, it is His words that define who we are. If we ever grasp that truth, then we no longer give anyone else permission to write the story of our lives. In fact, we take our pencil and begin to write His love on the hearts of others.[2]

When we hand the pencil to Christ, He rewrites all earlier messages and lessons:

Shame keeps you low, but forgiveness lifts you up.

Shame closes your eyes to possibilities, but forgiving shines the light to your potential.

Shame makes you a victim, but forgiveness leads you to help others find freedom.

How NASA Forgiveness Works

Candy's shame had nothing to do with her own deeds. She was a child bearing the adult-sized weight of her parent's choices. When we read Psalm 99, we glimpse an entire nation mired in shame. No individual person is highlighted, but what we do know from stories in Scripture is that in this group of people were many who continued in sin, as well as those who had committed no misdeeds. They lived justly and yet were swept into slavery due to the sins committed by their forefathers and their peers.

Once viewed by others as the apple of God's eye, the nation suffered indignities as slaves. They were beaten down as they labored under unfair and harsh conditions. They were mocked by nations that did not believe in their God, especially in light of their situation.

In the midst of their shame, we find the writer of Psalm 99 describing God as all encompassing, mighty, powerful. And that He comes down into the trenches to lift the shame from an entire nation: "LORD our God, you answered them; you were to Israel a forgiving [*nasa*] God" (Ps. 99:8). The word for forgiveness used here means "lifted up."

Including these deeper shades of meaning in the word "forgiveness," such as *armor bearer* and *lifted up*, hands the pencil to God. It doesn't erase the past, but it shifts the story to include God coming down into the trenches to erase shame from a person's life.

To feel shame is to feel bad about yourself. To feel conviction is to feel bad about what you've done. The first has no value. The second has great value.

When shame is not addressed, you may start to believe fundamentally that something is wrong with you. It's a feeling that can absolutely keep you trapped, not only in life, but as you choose relationships; as you try to be a people pleaser; as you confuse forgiveness with behaviors that have nothing to do with forgiving at all, like, allowing someone to treat you badly long-term because subconsciously you aren't sure you deserve to be treated with dignity or kindness.

It can also cause you to embrace lies as truth.

In her book *What Happens When Women Walk in Faith*, Lysa TerKeurst describes the lies that the enemy uses to kill our dreams. These lies also apply to shame and how it distorts the way that we see ourselves.

1. God couldn't care less about you.
2. God is too busy with the important people to be bothered by insignificant you.
3. God isn't to be trusted.
4. Death (speaking of failure or death of a dream) means defeat.
5. Dreams only happen by chance.[3]

For a moment, imagine the words you've heard spoken over you. Do they sound similar to any of the lies you've just read?

No one cares about you.

God must love others more because their life is better.

Did God forget me?

It's easier for others with better families/more money/better opportunities.

My dreams will never come true.

These are all lies, but due to the circumstances we embrace them, sometimes using them as a defense mechanism ("I'm this way because you did this") or worse, we allow these lies to keep us from discovering the vital truths further described by TerKeurst, which are:

1. God has a plan for me.
2. God is with me.
3. God will make a way.
4. God isn't surprised by death (of a dream).
5. God brings dreams to life.[4]

For a moment, think about the negative words you have heard said about you or to you. Write them down. Now mark an *X* through them. This is not who you are. Weigh the words in light of who spoke them. Remind yourself that the words were spoken out of someone else's pain or addiction or inability to love you as he or she should. If these words or actions formed your growing-up years, remind yourself that you are now an adult. You claim the words of adults when you are four because you have no other choice. But as an adult, you have the power to sift through those words and see them for what they are.

They are not truth. They are not yours to claim.

Now, allow God to lift you above the shame. Soak in the vital truths.

God has always had a plan for you.

His plan does not change, regardless of the choices of others. You can run from that plan, if you choose, but it's there in your DNA. If you had told me when I was a 16-year-old girl that God would one day allow me to travel the world sharing the gospel, or that I would be a radio co-host, or an author, I would have thought you insane.

But God saw the possibilities.

While I treasure my role in ministry, it is in the less visible roles that I find the greatest delight. He saw the capacity inside of me to live fully as His and find great satisfaction in my role as mom, mother-in-law, wife and gramma. My family, normal and chaotic and wonderful, is a treasure that I don't take for granted.

God promises that He is with you.

Was He with Candy when her mother left her alone to fend for herself? Yes. He was grieved, and we know that because over and over again in Scripture we see Jesus going out of the way to love a child or encourage His disciples that true love is caring for those who are defenseless. It's against His nature for a child to be emotionally orphaned.

God will make a way.

Is it okay to admit that you had it harder than many? I think so, because it's admitting the truth. But it becomes a hindrance when we profess that it will always hold us back, or it keeps us from discovering all that God has for us. Yes, the starting line is further back and the obstacles are bigger, but our challenges can also be our greatest assets. We don't take growth for granted. We delight in discovering what lies beyond the confines of our past. That's a slight shift in perspective that offers powerful incentive to transform.

That leaves the final two vital truths, which we'll combine. When we carry a burden of shame, we might not understand that it's okay to dream big. We take a huge step of faith, and there's a learning curve that comes with it. If we fall down, we might want to give up. But failure and obstacles are part of the journey, no matter where you begin. Consider the Olympic swimmer who walks to the edge of the high dive. How many times did she perform a belly buster instead of a swan dive in order to perfect her sport? How many bruises did it take?

God isn't surprised by failure, by missteps, by running into a wall that seems impossible to scale. It all comes with the journey. As we take those steps, believing in the truths rather than the lies, we begin to appreciate the journey as we develop character and re-silience and self-control as our dreams come to life, bringing joy along with it.

And what do you find along the way?

You find compassion.

When I drive to Colorado, I pull over to the craggy overhanging rocks along the highway; and when I step out, suddenly the countryside spans out as far I can see. It is such a different view from the winding road obscured by trees, asphalt and metal railings.

As Candy allowed God to take the shame she was never intended to bear, she began to see her growing-up years through different eyes. It didn't change the hardships she suffered, it simply added dimension. She could see deeper and further. She wasn't confined to the memories of a child, but pictured her past as an adult.

She recalls graduating from high school. She hoped to be able to attend a college that was beyond her means. One night, she left work and found a note on the windshield of her car. It read, "Candy, I got a job at your college, so now you can go for free." Her mother had signed up to clean dorms, which afforded her daughter a debt-free education.

In the midst of a lot of bad memories was a gift—a very generous gift of love from a mother to a daughter.

While Candy was in college, her mother started to climb out of addiction. A few years after Candy's graduation from college, her mother was clean from drugs. She was in a healthier relationship with a man and eventually remarried.

The act of forgiving allowed Candy to drop the all-bad or all-wrong label tagged to her mother. Her childhood was no longer completely defined by her mother's wrongdoing. Mixed in there were gestures of love and attempts to do the right thing.

Today, Candy's relationship with her mother' is a work in progress. They talk often on the phone. They went on a trip together. They tell each other that they love each other. Candy says, "God is healing us . . . together."

It's not perfect, and perhaps it never will be, but imperfect progress is a gift Candy has accepted.

Your Load Gets Lighter

In my book *The Mom I Want to Be*, I describe what it must have been like when I was born. There were no pink balloons, no baby showers with lemon petit fours and stacks of gifts. A 21-year-old woman stumbled down an alley, holding the hand of her three-year-old daughter, to find a pay phone. She gave birth in the hallway of the naval hospital. She brought her daughter home to poverty and uncertainty.

But God saw me.

That little wrinkled baby girl with brown hair was just as treasured as the girl in the bassinette next door with two loving parents. He saw my potential. He saw all the gifts and traits He had lovingly placed in my DNA. Shame was removed bit by bit over time as I embraced this truth and as I grew in my faith. The more I came to know God, the more I came to know me as well.

This relationship with God helps us to unpack the victim status. Perhaps the only difference between a victim and someone who is not is that we no longer go by that name.

If I hold on to bitterness because I wasn't given opportunities, I remain a victim.

If I blame my past for my sins, or my hurtful actions toward those I love, I remain a victim.

If I heap shame on others to make myself feel better, then I remain a victim.

But if I want to move forward, I "throw off everything that hinders" and I run with "perseverance the race marked out for us" (Heb. 12:1). I unpack shame and put on my running shoes every morning, inviting God into every aspect of my day. I unpack repeated behavioral patterns from the past (screaming, yelling, anything that hurt me that I am now doing to others) and I pack in resources that help me grow, sermons that spur me on, friends that cheer as I hit mile marker number 17 and the wind is blowing and it seems like I'm a bazillion miles from the finish line.

This packing and unpacking is intentional until it becomes natural. I don't reach for that unhealthy stuff, but rather I reach for God. That's when the real miracles begin.

We run the race, fully aware of our Armor Bearer running ahead of us, behind us, over us and around us, delighting in every step we take from shame to triumph.

YOUR STORY IMPACTS OTHERS

Candy is a counselor in middle school, and she says, "My story is not unique. There are children in every town who can identify with my story. There are children who are desperately trying to hide the secrets in their homes, and they wear their shame every single day. They come to school and put on a brave face and try hard to fit in. Many fall into addictions like their parents' before they even get a start in life."

She considers it a privilege to work with children who feel unwanted and unclean. Her colleagues believe that she is intuitive, but she knows that her past allows her the privilege of reading between the lines. Every time she loves one of these children, her hope is that he or she will experience God's love through her.

Perhaps this is the most compelling benefit of *nasa* forgiveness. The past becomes a catalyst to come alongside others who are bound by their past. You understand what they are experiencing, but you also are a living example of what God can do when one hands Him the weight of shame to discover an unrestricted, unburdened heart.

JUST YOU AND GOD

1. David was blessed (lifted up or exalted) due to forgiveness. What do you hope to receive as God takes your burden of shame?

   _____

   _____

   _____

   _____

   _____

2. Candy handed the "pencil" to God to write her story. Who is holding your pencil? Share the reason(s) you are taking the pencil away from that person or circumstance.

   _____

   _____

   _____

3. An armor bearer's job in the Old Testament was to do these things for the one he protected:

   • Exalt and uplift as a loyal friend
   • Rescue in difficulty and hardship
   • Repel any kind of attack; especially to protect from behind
   • Keep watch while the one he protected rested
   • Protect from false accusations
   • Come to the aid of in spiritual combat

   Which of these is your prayer today? What would that look like in real life?

   _____

   _____

   _____

4. Describe how allowing God to become your armor bearer will change you or your thought life.

   _____

   _____

   _____

5. Read 2 Corinthians 5:17. If the old is passed away and you are a new creation, how much energy do you wish to devote to thinking about or being angry at the past? Name one way this same energy can be utilized in a fresh, new way today.

   _____

   _____

   _____

6. Write down the name of one person who is experiencing the same kind of circumstances as you did in your past. How can God release this person from shame to find a new identity in Christ? (We are often able to offer hope to others more easily than to ourselves. Now, write your own story. What has God done, and what can He do?)

_____

_____

_____

_____

_____

_____

NASA PRINCIPLE

Give your shame to God. It's not yours to carry any longer.

TO NASA FORGIVE

Hand God the pencil.

PRAYER

Father, I release into Your capable hands the words and actions that caused me to feel ashamed. I thank You that You see me as worthy and beautiful and whole. Today I give You the pencil to write my story and the next chapter of my life. I can't wait to see what You have to say.

Notes
1. John MacArthur, *The Freedom and Power of Forgiveness* (Wheaton, IL: Crossway Books, 2009), p. 191.
2. Connie Davis Johnson, "Who Holds the Pencil," Hearts at Home, www.hearts-at-home.org. Used by permission.
3. Lysa TerKeurst, *What Happens When Woman Walk in Faith* (Eugene, OR: Harvest House Publishers, 2005), p. 9.
4. Ibid.

6

You Start Fresh

In the shadow of my hurt, forgiveness feels like a decision to reward my enemy. But in the shadow of the cross, forgiveness is merely a gift from one undeserving soul to another.

Andy Stanley, *Enemies of the Heart*

Her smile and laugh are engaging. Sometimes her words surprise me, and sometimes they make me blush with her candor. She's tender, loving, silly (in a good way) and generous.

She worries that I drive too much. It's not unusual for me to put 45,000 miles on a car in a year. Her 20-year-old Cadillac still has less than 100,000 miles. For her, a drive to a city an hour away becomes an all-day adventure. She's one of the hardest-working women I've ever met. Though my house is tidy, I never have understood the joy in closet cleaning sprees or polishing cupboards until they shine.

She's my mother, and I love her.

I've been waiting to share this new chapter in our relationship for a long time. Our story has been told at conferences, in books, on my blog and shared one-on-one with women, in each case only with her permission. My hope in the beginning was that our story would encourage others about what God can do, and it has. My mother's courage in allowing me talk about our past has been extraordinary. I asked her permission for the first book, and she granted it. But let's be honest. It's challenging to speak about the past without talking about the tougher parts.

That's why I'm so excited about this chapter. It contains the *after* parts.

It is my story of how God can help a person start fresh with someone who has been changed by His love. Even if he or she is still a work in progress. Even with the baggage of the past between you. Even if you have to hash out the hard parts to find a new relationship based on today instead of yesterday.

My mother and I long ago moved beyond the chapters of my childhood, because I've been an adult for a long time. My life and the decisions I've made in the past 30 years have been of my own choice. The dysfunction we struggled through was a season, a really bad season, and one that shaped both of us, but it was a season nonetheless. It's not that I've forgotten the past or that I pretend it doesn't exist; but there are so many more words that need to be included in our very public story. Our everyday relationship is whole; it has blossomed into a friendship and a strong mother-daughter connection—all because of forgiveness.

> ***rpk*** [Greek]: translated *kaphar:* (1) to cover; (2) to make atonement for; (3) to make reconciliation; (4) to purge.

RECONCILIATION

In *kaphar* forgiveness, the past is purged or pitched so that reconciliation can begin. This word is more complicated than some of the others we are exploring, because it means "atonement," a word that means to satisfy, amend or compensate for an injury or wrong.

Other words included in *kaphar* forgiveness are "to cleanse" and "purge." In the Old Testament, *kaphar* atonement [or forgiveness] was linked to rules and rituals.

If you've read the book of Leviticus, you might think like I do: *How in the world did these people do this?*

They separated wool from linen in their ephod (a garment worn during biblical times); slaughtered oxen, lambs and doves; ate or drank or abstained from certain foods and beverages. Men wore a hairy beard, and women covered their heads during prayer.

Tradition can be a beautiful expression of faith, but the problem with this type of atonement in the Old Testament was that it was so prohibitive that the divide between God and man was almost impenetrable.

Sometimes the divide between you and someone who has created havoc in your life may seem impossible to overcome. You have memories that shaped the way you viewed that person. And when someone like my mom, who regrets deeply her brokenness and how it affected her loved ones, apologizes, and it's not accepted, there's no way to atone for those wrongs. She can't undo her wrong by herself.

That's where *kaphar* forgiveness comes in to create a fresh start.

Paul joyfully proclaimed, "For if, when we were enemies, we were reconciled to God by the death of his Son, much more, being reconciled, we shall be saved by his life. And not only so, but we also joy in God through our Lord Jesus Christ, by whom we have now received the atonement" (Rom. 5:10-11, *KJV*).

In this verse, Paul was referring to the new version of *kaphar* forgiveness. It wasn't tied to ritual. It wasn't a list of rules. Up until this single New Testament mention of *kaphar*, this word meant something entirely different. But it changed because Jesus did what man couldn't do. He satisfied God's price for sin and closed the gap between man and God. The word "atonement" became "reconciliation" after Jesus entered the picture.

Because of the cross, we are reconciled to God. We are reconciled to each other. The impossible task becomes possible!

WHAT DOES THIS LOOK LIKE IN REAL LIFE?

I began the process of forgiving long before my mother was healed, because I needed it for my own healing and for my children's sake. But the day came when it was time to take a deeper step of forgiveness. It was time to reconcile our differences openly—to take our relationship from the past to present.

Combining atonement and reconciliation is a purge. A new slate. A new beginning. But the tricky part about reconciliation is that we often try to do it the Old Testament way. We create a long

list of rules or we keep that person at arm's length, or it's so complicated because of the mix of the old and the new that we just can't
seem to connect.

So how do you *kaphar* forgive?

REFRAME YOUR RELATIONSHIP

In his book *Hope in the Face of Conflict*, Dr. Kenneth C. Newberger, says
that we begin reconciliation through reframing our relationship.

> Framing relates to the way we perceive things, someone or
> something, in a good light or a negative one. Reframing
> refers to a change in an earlier perception. One comes to
> see the same situation or another person in a different way.
> It can have a transformative impact.[1]

As I interviewed my mom for my book *The Mom I Want to Be:
Rising Above Your Past to Give Your Kids a Great Future*, the parts of her
life where I was not included came to life. I started to see her separately from my childhood.

She was a premature baby born at two pounds and with un-
derdeveloped lungs into a home of chain smokers. She was the
child who dragged her foot when she walked down the street, hoping to gain attention from those who watched, because she felt
overlooked in her own home. She was a child molested at five, and
who had to testify in court against the older man who had enticed
her with ice cream. She was a teenager who became a wife and
mother at 15. She was the girl who lost her oldest child to cystic fi-
brosis when her baby was only two. She was the woman who left
the young, abusive sailor to find shelter, only to be sexually assaulted by him when he found her.

Reframing didn't make our past suddenly rose-colored, but it
did give me insight into the woman and mom she became. It helped
me see the brokenness she brought into the family dynamics.

It also helped me understand her courage.

Fifteen years old. Can you imagine? Losing her child at 17. No, I
can't go there. It's too painful to think about; but it was her reality.

Because of our childhood, some of us are so angry that we stopped communication once we left home. Some of us keep our moms at arm's length, because how can you trust someone who hurt you in the past? Another loves her mom for who she is while dealing with her own scars from the past.

I often share that my family tree is a gnarled mess, and it is. One broken woman after another handing down the legacy they had received, hoping that their children might do something better with it. When I prayed for a new branch of my family tree, my hope was that it would happen through me for my children and their children; and with God's help it has. But my mom sprouted some new shoots off of a forked branch as well.

Kaphar forgiveness allows me to see that.

Recently, my daughter gave my mom a Mother's Day card. My children know of our past, but it isn't relevant. Their memories are based on the relationship I have with my mother now. They've seen the growth, and they know what God has done. But in a professional classroom setting, my daughter, who is a professor, was asked to share about the women in her life. As she talked, parts of my mother's story began to powerfully impact her. She thought about it for days afterward, especially the story of my conception.

My biological father was physically abusive. My mother fled after baby number two (and the loss of baby number one) and moved in with a girlfriend. Her estranged husband showed up at the door with roses and kind words, and she invited him in. As soon as he made it through the door, he asked her to have sex, and she said no. He grabbed her, beat her with the thorny roses, sexually assaulted her on the stairs of the small garage apartment and then left. She discovered that she was pregnant six weeks later.

I was that child.

It would have been far easier, even in those days, to have chosen abortion. She was a young mom with no finances other than what she received from ironing for others and cleaning homes. Her mother had made it clear that she was not to return home, regardless of the circumstances.

In the Mother's Day card, my daughter wrote: "Meemaw, I want to thank you for how strong you are, and for the choice to keep my mom. You gave her life, and that gave me life."

While I had shared bits and pieces of those sentiments with my mother, it was my own daughter who expressed it in a way that affirmed the courageous choices my mother made when she was nearly a child herself. It caused me to question why I hadn't done that. Perhaps it is because my daughter can only see today. There are no embedded memories of dysfunction in her response. She sees my mother for who she is.

As I started fresh, my prayer became to purge—not the memories, because they are part of my story, but the emotions tied to those memories.

Father, help me clearly see the woman she is today. Take off the restraints of the past. Purge the emotions that no longer reflect the woman standing in front of me. Help me see her smile. Help me see how hard she tries. Help me treasure her touch, which seems unfamiliar at times, and yet she's reaching with arms to hold a daughter she loves. Help me love her back like You love me.

Over time, those prayers became reality. Not instantly, and not all at once. Layer by layer, the past was lifted to reveal a new relationship.

Have you reframed your view of the person with whom you desire to start fresh? Have you acknowledged the good parts? If so, have you expressed that to the person? The apostle Paul tells us:

> So we have stopped evaluating others from a human point of view. At one time we thought of Christ merely from a human point of view. How differently we know him now! This means that anyone who belongs to Christ has become a new person. The old life is gone; a new life has begun! (2 Cor. 5:16-17, *NLT*).

My mother has changed. My prayer is that one day all of her loved ones will see her through that transformation and reconcile their view of her with who she is today.

Perhaps reframing makes you feel that you are saying what happened is okay, something we've already discussed. But it merits a second look. In his book *Hope in the Face of Conflict*, Dr. Newberry wrote:

> In settings involving conflict, reframing doesn't change who the other person is or what the other person has done. It simply changes the way the aggrieved party views that person or behavior. Reframing is, among other things, whereby the wrongdoer can be regarded as someone over and above the wrong he has committed, a means of separating the wrongdoer from the wrong he has done.[2]

It's perfectly okay to admit that it's challenging to start over in a relationship when your history is tangled with painful memories.

STARTING FRESH, YOUR PART

The past can linger as an unspoken, but clearly felt, barrier in your relationship. This can cause you both, no matter how much progress you've made, to fall into the ugly dance of the past as you relate or interact with each other.

Let's be candid. Starting fresh when your history involves abuse or dysfunction can launch trust issues. If that person changed once and relapsed, you may not be willing to try again.

There are also communication problems. What can you talk about? And what can you not talk about? What topics lie just below the surface and can explode like a landmine when you unexpectedly tiptoe past a hidden line?

Everyday imperfections are often magnified. An off day, a loss of temper, a bad choice—all of these might signal to you that your loved one is unstable or untrustworthy. It makes sense, because that's what happened in the past.

Your brain signals it could happen again, because it *did* happen once. This fails to account for the fact that everyone has off days. We all lose our tempers and make mistakes. It also sends the message to a loved one that perfection is required and there is zero tolerance for error. It's life without parole for both of you. Your growth is stunted as you react, respond and relate with that person as if you were still a child or entangled in the past.

So, how do you create a new way of relating?

You create a new groove.

Let me explain. Not long ago, I rode a bus through the Swiss Alps between Austria and Italy. It was snowing, though it was spring. The mountainside was majestic. Thirteenth-century fortress-like dwellings jutted out of the mountainside above, and small farms dotted the valley below. Waterfalls spilled down from the mountaintop, and the snowcapped mountains reached into the clouds. It was the waterfalls that captured my attention. Somehow, though snow covered the vast mountaintops, the water knew where to go. It didn't rush down the entire mountain; it followed familiar paths carved over generations.

Our brains are much like those waterfalls. We create familiar grooves in our brains. We have our go-tos. When we get angry or feel bad, we respond in a certain way. When we get defensive, we respond in a common pattern. So, when we relate to that person who once caused us pain, we fall into a familiar groove.

In the Alps, if you move one large rock, suddenly the water has room to go in a new direction. It will, at first, go toward the old, deeply grooved path it always follows; but over time, a new path will emerge. A little wider. A little deeper.

You and I, with God's help, can form a new groove in our brains. But it's not going to feel normal at first. It's a conscious choice rather than a natural response. We begin to respond in a different way. We begin to see that person in a new light. Over time, the new groove becomes deeper and more of a natural response while the old groove—left dry and unfilled—dries up.

A New Rhythm in Your Relationship

Reconciliation in itself is like a dance in the beginning.

You expect disappointment.

Harsh words and lashing out have always been the way you've communicated.

You are used to walking on eggshells.

It's what you have grown to expect; and yet, now that person is showing up when she says she will. She is doing what she promised. She responds with grace or an attempt at grace. She isn't perfect, but she is different, and it's hard to know what to do.

In a sense, you are waiting for her to mess up.

That is awkward at best.

I understand awkward. My husband (sorry, babe) has no rhythm, but that doesn't mean he doesn't love to dance. When he first approaches me with his untraditional dance moves, I laugh every time. I can't help it! If everyone else is moving to the right, my husband is going to bust a move to the left, and do it with enthusiasm. I don't try to correct him anymore; I just go with it and have fun.

Maybe you aren't sure whether to go right or left. It takes time to develop a rhythm that works together.

A couple of years ago, my mother was in the hospital. She suffers from chronic asthma, and every winter the battle gets fierce. When she was admitted to the hospital and treated with heavy doses of steroids and medication, I received an unintelligibly frantic phone call from my mother and raced to the hospital. She rose from the bed and tumbled across the room, crying.

I recognized the old dance moves. They were all there.

Weeping.

Depression.

Anger.

Lashing out.

Out of control.

"I'm doing it again," she said. Even in the fog of medicine she recognized the instability.

For just a second, old memories flooded in from the past. But only for a moment. I put my hands on my mom's shoulders. I wish I could explain that beautiful moment as I stood there with my hands on her shoulders. The past fell away. Yes, I recognized the instability; but as an adult she and I had a new relationship. When I was a kid, she had screamed for help and no one had listened.

That was a dance move from the past that *I* could change.

I explained that the medicine was making her feel out of control. "We're right here. Dad is here. Mindy and Ron and Randy are on their way. I'm here," I said, pulling her close. "You don't have to be strong right now. You just have to get better. The medicine is clearing up your lungs, but it's also making you feel like this. It's going to get better."

If I had remained stuck in the dance of the past, I would have felt threatened. But as an adult, I had noted all of the changes—the strength—in my mom. Because of reframing *her* past, I recognized the fear that overwhelmed her at a situation beyond her control.

That changed everything! She felt safe; I didn't feel threatened. We truly knew each other for who we are today.

Reconciliation Covers

In *kaphar* forgiveness, one meaning is "to cover." This describes a covering like tar pitch used to waterproof a roof in those days. (In the Old Testament, Moses' mother used tar and pitch to waterproof the papyrus basket in which she placed her son to hide him from danger.) Tar and pitch is sticky and hard to handle; but when it is put on a roof and cured by the sun, it is impenetrable. It keeps the elements out and the people underneath the roof safe.

The more I let go of my past relationship with my mother, the safer she felt. While my forgiving was instrumental in my healing, it also released my mother to take her own steps. There is an old expression: "You and I do not see things as they are. We see things as *we* are." As time passed, my mother began to see herself without a mirror of guilt. She was able to honestly admit her errors of the past but accept the covering atonement that only God could give.

It's not your responsibility to make a person whole again. It's an impossible task. Understanding how they arrived at their brokenness gives you insight, but not a license to try to *fix* your loved one.

Reframing the past also allowed the covering of healing to shelter me. It set me free to seek God as my need-meeter rather than trying to find that in another human being, or resent it when she couldn't measure up to my expectations or what I saw in others. Reframing helps you see where the other person lost her way. But instead of trying to put that person on the path you think she should be on, focus on your own dance moves.

QUESTIONS ONLY YOU CAN ANSWER

Kaphar forgiveness gives your relationship a crack at a second chance and frees you from trying to bear the burden of changing anyone but yourself. It also allows you to ask important questions and reestablish your relationship based on the answers.

Has my loved one changed?

If the answer is yes, take an honest look at why you may still be struggling. If it's trust issues, then identify those. There have been conversations where I have had to say, "This isn't you. This is my issue. I'm still struggling in this area, but I'm working on it." That's an honest response that allows me to take responsibility for my part in the reconciliation.

It's okay to take baby steps. On television, reconciliation is painted as this magical moment where everyone walks away arm in arm; but when the cameras go away, reality hits. Reconciliation takes time and prayer and working through conflict to start fresh. The relationship is worth it, and over time those issues lessen, get resolved and heal.

Surprise that person. Let him or her know that you see and appreciate transformation. And while you are doing that, there's a little bit of transformation going on inside of you too.

ARE YOU EXPECTING PERFECTION?

Perfection is not going to happen, and we set ourselves up for failure when we expect it. There are things that haven't changed with my mom. They are small. One is that my mom struggles with negativity. That's hard, at times, for an over-the-top optimist.

One day, we were in the car together. I had driven to Tulsa to hang out. My mom *loves* quality time. We went out to lunch and were on our way to a movie. I had listened for almost an hour to a pretty negative conversation. She had every right to share her thoughts, and negative thoughts are sometimes necessary to air out. But this was more than that; it was depressing, and it was causing me to feel resentment.

At that point, I had a choice. I could remain silent and frustrated. I could lash out. I could sigh a martyr's sigh and think: *Why did I even make this effort?*

Each of us has daily choice points in every relationship, but we encounter more of them with someone with whom we are trying to reconcile. Some of our everyday choices are random; others are weighty. These decisions lead us in one direction or another.

"Mom?"

"Yes, hon."

I gently asked if we could change the topic. I let her know that I was excited to be with her, but that I'd love to talk about our day together or any other topic she'd like to share. To my mother's credit, she signed up! She didn't realize how the negativity was creating a barrier in our good day until I spoke up. I wish I could say I handle every choice point that way, but sometimes I fail. It's my prayer that I'll remember how much those choice points matter, especially with my mom.

You see, our choice points don't just affect us, they affect those within the vicinity of our decisions, throwing them into a choice point of their own. If I had lost it with my mom, I would have waltzed into an old, unhealthful dance pattern, and both of us would have been stuck twirling away.

Are you willing to alter your responses to imperfections as you acknowledge that you have your own quirks and work-in-progress behavior?

EVERY RELATIONSHIP IS DIFFERENT

Perhaps you are early in the process of *kaphar* forgiving. You acknowledge that a loved one has changed, or that he or she is working hard toward reconciliation; or perhaps the trust issues are huge because reconciliation has just begun.

What can you do?

Learn the Art of the Pause

The other day, a friend of mine rushed at me with open arms. I hadn't seen her in several days, and I playfully drew my leg and arms into a Karate Kid posture in defense. We had a great laugh, but honestly, there are times where I feel someone "rushing at me" in a less positive way and I do the same thing emotionally.

When this happens, the person may not even realize what you are feeling, and yet you are taking a defensive posture or grabbing your verbal sword. Step back for a moment and pause to let the defensive instincts settle down. If your instinct is to lash out or say something you'll regret you've given that instinct a break.

Believe the Best

Have you ever said something because you felt rushed, were hurting from something or someone else or just flat-out spilled out your words without thinking? I have. Believing the best means that we provide some depth to the situation. We look past the words or the action to the person beneath. What was his or her motivation? If it wasn't to intentionally harm, that means we offer a little grace, the same grace we hope to receive when our words come out all wrong.

Believing the best means that you truly see the other person without the filter of yesterday. It's a place of equality and dignity that only *kaphar* forgiveness offers, not just to them but to you as well.

Ask for Wisdom

God offers it willingly. In Psalm 51: 6, we find these comforting words. "Behold, You desire truth in the innermost being; and in the hidden part You will make me know wisdom" (*NASB*).

But there's more: "If any of you lacks wisdom, you should ask God, who gives generously to all without finding fault, and it will be given to you" (Jas. 1:5).

You aren't without help in your choice points. You can go with feelings and rash reactions, or you can invite your heavenly Father into the situation and into the relationship.

You can ask Him for the right words. These are words that are not accusatory. They are honest, but not pointed. They affirm the relationship. They are words that show that you are listening, and you hear what the other person is trying to say.

You can ask God to show you the right timing. For my mom and me, those moments have been mostly unscheduled. Some of them have been painful. Others were moments when I walked away surprised by her insight. There were moments that I gained a new picture of her as she shared her side of the story, something I could not consider as a child. But as an adult, it helped me gain clarity.

You can ask for help to sort through your emotions to find insight into the real issues—which allows you to work through the problem with purpose rather than attack.

MAKE AMENDS

Finally, as you look at your part in reconciliation, you know there are times when you mess up. If the choice you made is the choice you wish you hadn't in your new relationship, there is power in a sincere apology. To make amends is to offer more than simply words. It means repairing the rift you created in the moment.

THE POWER OF RECONCILIATION

I know my mom will read this. She carries copies of *The Mom I Want to Be* with her, even though it contains the harsher descriptions of what we went through as a family. When she runs out of those copies, she asks for more. She loves nothing more than telling people that this is our story, that God has healed her Suzie and God has given her a fresh start.

Recently, in one of my mom's sick times, I sat beside her in a room while she slept. She was propped up on pillows. She was exhausted from the steroids that helped her bronchial tubes open but dished out side effects of insomnia, manic activity and launched her on a hair-trigger emotional roller coaster. She had finally fallen asleep with the help of a pretty heavy-duty sleeping pill.

While I sat beside her, bittersweet emotions flooded me. Love. Fear—because this was the third time for her to be so ill in a year. Uncertainty about the severity of her labored breathing.

But it went deeper. There was also regret over the years I struggled to forgive our past; over the brokenness that went on in my mother's life for more years than she wished. I felt sadness for how few years it seemed we had ahead of us in this new phase, though we have been in it for more than two decades.

Suddenly, I felt her fingertips on my hand. She reached and closed in around my fingers. Her hands were soft, her fingers bent from arthritis. "I love you, babes," she whispered.

I said it then, and I say it now.

I love you too, Mom. I'm so grateful for the opportunity to tell the rest of our story. And I'm glad you got better. Somehow, in spite of your health problems, you are back to your cleaning-the-cupboards-frenzied self, and that makes me smile.

Maybe This Is the Painful Part

Perhaps your loved one is no longer in the picture, or it seems like you'll never hit the *kaphar* phase of forgiveness, like I have with my mom. One woman reading the manuscript sent back this chapter with these words: "I can't read this". "It's like a kid with 50 cents looking in a jewelry store window. I'll never have that."

I shared with her that I had experienced what she's feeling. Yes, I know what it is to work toward a fresh start and to actually receive it. I also know what it is for that door to shut firmly, even as I offered a fresh start. My biological father's last words as I reached out were, "I don't even know if you are mine." I also know what it is to choose to remain in a chaotic relationship with a loved one as I work toward my own fresh start, regardless of this individual's choice to heal or change.

Kaphar forgiveness can take place in all of these situations. It's not unusual to carry a burden of unforgiveness long after someone has died or they've continued in their behavior and you've had to shut the door on the relationship to stay safe; or they've changed and want to begin again.

Reconciliation doesn't always mean a one-to-one personal encounter; it can mean "coming to an understanding," even if no one else signs up. That in itself can powerfully lead to an unburdened heart as you *kaphar* forgive.

Just You and God

1. Describe the characteristics of the person you are struggling to forgive. Now differentiate between yesterday and the present. Are these current traits, or are they from the past? How many of the characteristics no longer reflect what the person has become?

_____

_____

_____

_____

_____

_____

2. Atonement means satisfaction, compensation or amends given for an injury or wrong. List one thing you believe (or have believed in the past) would satisfy the wrong you suffered.

_____

_____

_____

_____

_____

_____

3. List ways that you have grown or changed in the past few years. How would you like others to acknowledge those changes?

_____

_____

_____

_____

_____

_____

4. Read Psalm 103:12. How does this verse show you how to forgive and start fresh?

_____

_____

_____

_____

_____

_____

5. In Luke 4:18, Jesus stated that He came to set the captive free. How will starting fresh, with Christ's help, set all parties free from the heavy burden of unforgiveness?

_____

_____

_____

_____

_____

_____

6. Reconciliation may not be possible in person, but how does reconciling the past (or coming to an understanding) bring peace?

_____

_____

_____

_____

_____

_____

KAPHAR PRINCIPLE

Reconciliation is possible through Christ.

TO KAPHAR FORGIVE

Separate the memories of the past from who the person is today
to begin the process of reconciliation.

PRAYER

Lord, I'm stuck in the memories and emotions of the past. I've tried to make others pay, or I've tried to change my view of what they should be. Today, I step back for a new glimpse of who they are becoming, with your help. Will you help me as I take steps toward a fresh start?

Notes

1. Dr. Kenneth C. Newberger, *Hope in the Face of Conflict: Making Peace with Others the Way God Makes Peace with Us* (Three Sons Publishing SDM, 2009), p. 134.

2. Ibid., p. 135.

7

You Experience a Role Reversal

To forgive is to set a prisoner free and discover that the prisoner was you.

Lewis B. Smedes

In 1962, she entered the world as Baby Salvatore. Four days later, she left the hospital in the arms of two loving parents, known from that moment forward as mom and dad. She grew up loved, but unfortunately, from the age of three until just before her twelfth birthday, that concept of love was skewed by repeated assaults perpetrated by two family members.

When she entered her teens, Stephanie says, "I started giving myself away."

She became pregnant, then married. By the time she was 19, she was divorced and a single mom. At 21, she married again. She became single again at 22. Stephanie says she could have posed as the poster child for the song, "Looking for Love in All the Wrong Places," which is where she met her next husband. He was the drummer in a band at a local bar. She was smitten. They started dating, and soon she was pregnant again. They married, and their son was born six months later.

Stephanie was in her early twenties when she started to consider the claims of Christ for the first time. It was also the first time she began to think about what had happened to her. When you are molested from the age of three, your perception of normal gets skewed. She had bought into the lie that she was only valuable to others when she gave herself physically to them. Yet here was a God who loved her for who she was, at the point where she was, and whose love was pure.

According to Stephanie, "Jesus reached down, captured my heart and radically changed a broken girl with a bad past and a bleak future."

It was as if all the pieces, her choices and the choices of others, were melted down and reformed to put back onto the wheel, where the hands of the Potter began to gently reshape and restore her to her original beauty. She wanted nothing more than to live for Him. For the first time, she felt forgiven and clean.

Several months after her conversion, her husband followed. Though her life was now on a different course, the past was rising in a new way. She had never allowed herself to feel deeply before. She was experiencing the love of her Savior. She deeply loved her two children and her husband. She was learning to love herself. But these good feelings also meant that she was experiencing post-traumatic memories, realizing for the first time how hurt she must have been as a little girl, and how far the acts of her abusers had led her away from what should have been a blessed life.

These acts of her abusers also hindered her from having a "normal" relationship with her husband, something they were working through. Many of her childhood memories had disappeared. And as a defense mechanism, she had learned how to push through life without feeling rather than experience joy and love and a full range of emotions. It made her angry when she considered the choices she didn't get to make, like whether or not she would be a virgin when she married.

She mourned the fact she never had the chance just to be a little girl. As she reflected on what had really taken place, she was angry for the first time. Until that moment, she thought she had forgiven because she had moved on; but turning the page on sexual abuse is vastly different from dealing with those who violated your trust.

When They Aren't Asking for Your Forgiveness

The situation was further complicated because neither of the abusers had asked for her forgiveness. She confronted one of the family members, who showed no remorse. He offered excuses, but it was clear that he didn't believe he needed her forgiveness. She expressed her truth, and that was all she felt she could do, feeling that to bring it up again would be counterproductive.

That left the other abuser. In this case, there could be no excuses, as he was an adult when the abuse took place. Stephanie was in her thirties when she finally made that phone call, and in an awkward dialogue, Stephanie expressed what God had done in her life and that she wanted to verbally forgive him.

"I wondered if you would ever bring this up," he said. As they spoke, he acknowledged what he had done but didn't offer an apology.

Stephanie hung up the phone, knowing that it wasn't likely that an apology would ever come. It didn't. He later passed away.

Saying it out loud, in both cases, was more difficult than just moving on and letting it lie. Dealing with her abusers as an adult meant that for the first time she was really addressing what had happened and how it had left scars on her heart that not only altered what could and should have been an innocent childhood, but left her filtering her concept of love through a perverted lens.

When she felt God moving in to heal her, that's when she felt she had to forgive: her lost childhood and how that sexual abuse had marked a young woman who didn't have a clue that she was worth more than a sexual encounter. Stephanie says, "One of the wonderful things about the Lord is that He knows we need to be fully healed. He loves us enough to dredge up painful memories of our past in order to bring us to a place where we understand we need to forgive in order to experience the healing we so desperately need . . . even when we don't even know it."

There was something liberating about taking the difficult step of forgiving, even when her abusers didn't acknowledge their need or receive it, because forgiving was releasing the hold that abuse had created.

Forgiveness came in stages.

After her parents passed away, she once again was confronted with emotions and memories. Though she believes her father never knew, her mother knew of at least one of the abuser's actions. She had walked into a room shortly after young Stephanie was molested. She had tried to tell her mother what was going on, but her mother explained it away, refusing to believe that what her little girl was saying could be true. Later, Stephanie talked with her mother as an adult. Her mother put the brakes on the conversation. Stephanie believes the truth was too painful, and rather than listen, she pretended that it never happened.

In each instance, Stephanie went through the process of working through painful memories, with God's help. She no longer held on to those memories as her identity, and she didn't allow someone else's limitations to keep her from healing.

Today, Stephanie is a mom, wife, grandma and a strong, beautiful woman of faith. She mentors moms all over the nation. She is drawn to women who started their relationship with God in a vulnerable place. She is also drawn to moms who want to give their children a safe and loving home. She leads Bible studies and teaches women.

She often reflects on where she started, where she has been and what she has been through. It is her testimony. It is what God can do, and did, in her.

κρατέω translated *krateō* [Greek]: (1) hold onto; (2) take hold; (3) keep; (4) accomplish; (5) attain; (6) arrest.

KRATEŌ FORGIVENESS

In John 20, we find the disciples in hiding. Jesus had died, and that threw his family and the apostles into a whirlwind of fear and uncertainty. Some, like Peter, were so afraid that they gave in to fear (see Luke 22:54-62) and ran from their association with Christ.

They had reassembled in a small house, huddling there to regroup and think about what they would do next. The doors were tightly locked for fear of the Jewish leaders. They may have also been hiding together in fear that the authorities might accuse them of tampering with the body of Jesus in the event that something miraculous did take place.

Suddenly, Jesus was among them.

Though He had appeared to Mary Magdalene earlier, and she raced to tell them that their Savior was resurrected, they weren't certain of what was true or not.

But here Jesus stands, His hands outstretched. "Peace be with you!" (John 20:19) he says. He draws them to look at His hands and His side. They could clearly see the scars from the nails and the spear.

The disciples were overjoyed.

Jesus says it again, "Peace be with you!" but He adds, "As the Father has sent me, I am sending you" (v. 21).

And then He did something unusual: "And with that he breathed on them and said, 'Receive the Holy Spirit. If you forgive anyone's sins, their sins are forgiven; if you do not forgive them, they are not forgiven'" (vv. 22-23).

In that tucked-away house with locked doors, the disciples filled with fear, Jesus breathed on them, signifying the Holy Spirit being birthed into them so they didn't have to live in fear. They were free to live as Jesus had taught them.

And from that day forward, they did.

In fact, something so huge happened after that moment that these men went on to build churches and build up people. They were persecuted, but they didn't give up. They were respected and honored by others and were known as miracle workers and men of wisdom. They became brave leaders of a movement so powerful that Christianity goes on today. And in the end, all but one were martyred for their faith. John, the one who wasn't martyred, escaped death but, according to tradition, only after being isolated on an island and boiled in oil. The disciples were not only no longer afraid but willingly offered up their lives rather than turn away from their belief in Christ.

Their relationship with God far outweighed anything man could do to them.

KRATEŌ FORGIVENESS
CREATES A ROLE REVERSAL

Can you imagine it? You and I are talking, and all of a sudden I lean over and breathe on you. What would you think?

Jesus was leaving the disciples soon to join His heavenly Father. Though Jesus had tried repeatedly to prepare them for this moment, they were anything but. They hadn't understood Him when He spoke in times like those described in John 12:31-36, where He said, "My light will shine for you just a little longer. Walk in the light while you can, so the darkness will not overtake you. Those who walk in the darkness cannot see where they are going. Put your trust in the light" (vv. 35-36, *NLT*).

He had taught them all they needed to know, but they had been walking the earth with Him at their side. They watched Jesus perform miracles. They sat at His feet and listened to His teaching. Now it was time for them to *go*.

Time for them to come out of hiding. To stop being afraid. They had a job to do. There were miracles they would perform. Churches they would build. A message of hope they would share.

In John 20:22-23, we find this word *krateō* as Jesus spoke about forgiving. The deeper shades of meaning in this word are "to hold onto," "to keep," "to accomplish," and most importantly, "to release" so that something more powerful can take place in a person or situation.

The disciples needed all of the elements Jesus had just given. They needed peace in a fearful place and among people that caused harm, and with an uncertain future. They needed the power that only God Himself offers.

As they stepped out in ministry, these men would have to make decisions about forgiveness over and over again. They would choose, or not, to forgive the religious leaders who raised them as boys, but who now clamored for their arrest. They would choose, or not, to forgive each other as they tried to fulfill all that Jesus said they would do and yet stumbled into arguments or differing opinions. They would choose, or not, to accept God's grace when they fell short.

One commentator reminds us that Jesus wasn't giving the apostles a license to withhold forgiveness from anyone; he was reminding them that it was key as they stepped out to do the job God had for them.[1] They would march out of that room and see people healed, the gospel preached and lives transformed. The message of forgiveness was foundational in the gospel message.

They also had the privilege of sharing God's view on how a person can receive forgiveness: If you believe in Jesus, then there is rich forgiveness of your sins. If you reject Jesus' sacrifice, then you refuse that gift and are not forgiven. This same principle would apply as they made decisions in their own lives to forgive. It was foundational as they operated in the power of the Holy Spirit and followed Jesus' instructions to love each other as He had loved them.

Because of this act in John 20, there was a role reversal among the frightened disciples. Here's what they moved away from and moved toward:

From fear to faith.

From hiding to harboring a light so bright it couldn't help but be seen.

From being confused to being compelled.

It was a key that unlocked their potential, no matter how challenging it was to initially walk outside those locked doors to find their destiny.

I bless you with peace.

I give you power.

Forgive.

When you are sexually abused, as Stephanie was, you can close yourself off in a solitary place. Who can I trust? Does God still have a plan for me? Is everything He spoke about my destiny still true? That's often a place of uncertainty and apprehension. What Christ offered the disciples was a blessing. Throughout Scripture a blessing is, in essence, a go-ahead from another.

Move out from your hiding place.

You don't have to live in fear anymore.

I offer you peace.

Suzanne Eller

Jesus also offers you power through the Holy Spirit. In Romans 8:1-2, Paul describes how the hold of sin is broken and we find freedom through Christ. If we read about this freedom and see it only as freedom from our own sinful acts, we might miss the complete message. Through Christ, we are offered freedom from the hold of *all* sin, whether that is due to another person's sin or our own. We (you and me) are not destined to be bound by the influence of another person's choices!

Finally, we are reminded of the gift of forgiveness that releases the hold for all who live in it, whether we are offering it or receiving it.

What happens when that hold is released?

You Are Released to Hear His Voice

My friend and I were driving to the airport. As we drove, I shared discouragement over some news I had just received about a young woman I had known for several years. She had given birth to two babies by two different men, and now she was with a third man. He had left a comment on Facebook that was demeaning and crude, and I was heartbroken that she couldn't see how little he valued her as a woman.

I felt as if something was broken with her "picker." The worse a guy treated her, the more she seemed drawn to him. She would describe all of his virtues, though it was clear that meeting a guy on Facebook who was still married and fresh out of jail wasn't the best match.

"I don't get it," I said. "She deserves better, but she can't seem to understand that."

"Something has happened to her," my friend replied after several moments. Then she shared her own story, one similar to Stephanie's. She said that after she was sexually abused, it led her to jump full-fledged into any relationship that made her feel good, if only for a moment. For several years, she was wedged in that role. She suggested that my young friend might be stuck in that same place.

"Don't give up on her," she said.

Though I was frustrated, I hadn't planned on giving up. But the insight my friend provided helped me pray in a whole new way. You see, Jesus sees what I cannot, and for a moment I had forgotten that. Our Savior continually confounded others because He sought out those that others had given up on.

Most weren't even seeking Him, but He was certainly searching for them.

Did you notice that one of the first people to bump into Jesus after the resurrection was Mary Magdalene? She was once one of the most shattered women in the Bible. She was trapped in torment, but Jesus loosed her from the hold of demons that wouldn't let go (see Luke 8:2). After her healing, Mary Magdalene had her own role reversal.

She became Jesus' friend. She was known as a strong woman of faith, and her good works were visible in the ministry.

When Jesus hung on the cross, and strong men ran for their lives, Mary was kneeling not far from the cross. Her Savior had met her in her greatest hour of need, and she was with Him at His most vulnerable hour.

When Jesus met Mary Magdalene in the garden, after His resurrection, she ran to the disciples to share her news. While they were locked away in fear, she remained by the tomb, waiting. This can only mean one thing. She had heard every word Jesus spoke as she sat at His feet. She was not hiding because she was waiting for Him to emerge triumphant from the grave, just as He said He would.

When Jesus freed her from her torment, she had more than a Sunday-morning church experience. She was loosed in such a measure that she knew with certainty that this was the Savior. She listened to every word that fell from His lips as He spoke about the cross and the fact that He would rise after three days. When she saw Him in the garden, she rushed toward Him, arms open with an embrace.

Some of the most profound women of faith, like Stephanie and my friend, are that way because of their personal encounter with Christ. They live out the truth that "whom God sets free, He sets free indeed!" (see John 8:36). Their relationship with Him isn't casual;

it is one of listening and responding to His voice. They embrace that love and can't wait to race to others to share what He has done.

YOU ARE RELEASED TO HAVE A FUTURE

For Stephanie, forgiving meant that she stopped looking in the rearview mirror. She had goals. Dreams. People to love. Life to live. She says, "I refuse to hide my past in a neatly wrapped Christian package stamped 'holy'; but I also believe that there is no one too battered, too broken, too dirty, too unlovable, too unworthy or too unforgivable for God. Our value isn't based on what we have to offer or what others have done to us. We are defined by what Christ has done for us."

Sexual abuse doesn't lead everyone in the same direction. You may not identify with Stephanie's words, but the core message is that you are relabeled from the effects of the abuse to your real self, which allows you to carve out your own path.

Shannon Ethridge, author, speaker and lay counselor, wrote in *The Sexually Confident Wife* that her uncles sexually molested her. For many years she struggled with what took place, but she wasn't sure how to define it. She came up with this definition:

> The word abuse can be best understood by breaking it down into syllables: ab-use or ab(normal)-use. In other words, to abuse something is to use it for a reason other than its intended purpose. When you were abused you were used for something other than for what you were intended. You, as a healthy female, were intended to some-day experience and enjoy a healthy sense of sexuality. Don't let someone else's gross error become your own. Don't continually look at yourself through the lens that your abuser once looked through. Remember who you are, and know that someone else's misusing you to satisfy his own selfishness doesn't negate or change who you really are as a valuable human being who is worthy of love and deserving of sexual pleasure.[2]

What happens in sexual abuse isn't normal, nor is it ever acceptable. Forgiving the abuser isn't saying that it is normal or acceptable. It's not saying that you don't prosecute; we don't want others to be harmed in the same way.

But pardoning sin isn't our role, it's God's (and we'll dig deeper into that in a later chapter); but *krateō* forgiving helps you to separate another person's actions from the way you and God perceive yourself. Sexual abuse is what happened to you, not who you are.

Father, release the hold that sexual abuse placed on my heart.

Father, replace the message I embraced as truth.

Father, loose the fear and lack of trust that was conceived.

I am beautiful and whole and healed because of Your touch on my life.

The abuser is never beyond God's forgiveness, but *krateō* forgiveness means that as the Master breathes over and into your life, God works out *His* forgiveness, according to heaven's principles, in the lives of your abusers. They may never seek your forgiveness or want God's, but if they do, there is healing for them as well.

But you step fully into today and tomorrow regardless of your abuser's response.

You Are Released to Pour into Others

Two little girls live across the street from me. One is five and the other is younger than two. When I water my flowers, the two little girls and their dog often run over to hang out. Trinity, the five-year-old, picks flowers and puts them in my hair. Maci, the toddler, picks them and tries to make it over to me without pulverizing them. She rarely does and holds out the crushed purple petals with a look of disappointment.

We can hold so tightly to feelings associated with abuse or offense that they keep us from pouring into others. Trinity had learned how to take the beautiful flower, hold it lightly in her hand and give it away. It's this type of hold we see in *krateō* forgiveness. It's like a touch and release action. The hold on us is released as we hold tightly to God. That, in turn, allows us to freely pour out to others.

We read in Mark 1:31 that Jesus and His disciples left to eat and to rest after a long day. When they arrive, they discover that their hostess is sick with a high fever. Jesus goes to her bedside and takes her by the hand (*krateō*) and helps her sit up. At His touch the fever leaves.

The hold and release goes into effect. She stands up and then prepares a meal for them. She is free to minister to those around her out of the Master's touch on her life.

Have you ever heard that whisper, saying, "Be all that I know you can be," and you respond with, "But this is what happened, God"?

Some of my most meaningful moments in ministry have happened when I sit with a woman and she has prejudged me because of my pointy-toed shoes or the fact that I am a writer (big deal, right?), and after I hear her story, I share my own.

All the barriers fall away. We are now just two women whose stories intertwine. I love that moment when she realizes that I was a young girl, broken and angry, who even now is continually surprised and amazed at the love of my Savior.

In a sense, we are all Mary Magdalenes.

Do You Feel God Asking You to Forgive?

Perhaps, like Stephanie, you desire to verbalize forgiveness to your abusers as a testament to what God has done inside of you. We are often compelled to offer grace in many situations that others might not grasp. This is between you and God, and no one can ask you to take that step except for Him.

Most of the work that takes place begins in the heart, and at the right time it becomes an act of mercy. Ask the Holy Spirit to lead you. Pray for wisdom. If you have someone who is a trusted and spiritual mentor, let that person guide you through the process. Never, ever put yourself or your loved ones in a place of jeopardy. If you take this step and it's not accepted or needed, understand that the response does not hinder you from running after all that God has for you as He breathes peace and power and purpose over your life.

JUST YOU AND GOD

1. Abuse is what someone did, not who you are. Write down five words that describe who you are as a person, separate from the past or the abuse.

_____

_____

_____

_____

2. What hold remains on your life due to abuse (of any kind)? Ask God to breathe peace, power and forgiveness into that hiding place. Make it a prayer.

_____

_____

_____

_____

3. Read Romans 8:1-3. If you belong to Him, you are free from the power of sin, even if it's another person's sin. How do these verses give you hope?

_____

_____

_____

4. Read John 8:36. What does this verse mean to you personally?

_____

_____

_____

_____

5. How would you like to pour out to others as God pours healing into your life?

   _____

   _____

   _____

   _____

6. Each of the people mentioned who turned to Jesus had a "role
   reversal." What would/does a role reversal look like for you?

   _____

   _____

   _____

   _____

KRATEŌ PRINCIPLE

The hold of sin is released, and a role reversal takes place.
You are free to be who God made you to be.

TO KRATEŌ FORGIVE

Invite His peace and power into the hiding places.

PRAYER

*My Savior, You continually sought out those who might otherwise hide
from You because of their brokenness. You bring peace where it might not
otherwise exist. You breathe power into my life simply because You know
me, and You know what I can do, with Your help. Help me to release the
hold that abuse placed on my life. I offer it up to You today. Take it.
I don't want it, and it's not who I am anymore.*

Notes

1. John F. Walvoord and Roy B. Zuck, *The Bible Knowledge Commentary: An Exposition of the Scriptures* (Wheaton, IL: Victor Books, 1985), John 20:21-23.
2. Shannon Ethridge, *The Sexually Confident Woman* (New York: Three Rivers Press, 2009), p. 50.

8

You Find a Safe Place

Think about that. The grief you are suffering as a result of loss has already been borne by Jesus. The sorrows you are feeling from a broken heart have already been borne by Him. The wounds you so want healed have already been taken care of.

Cindi McMenamin, *When a Woman Overcomes Life's Hurts*

Sometimes we are led to believe that when we forgive, everything falls into place.

But what if you don't have your happily ever after?

MarLo was 17, and a senior in high school when she met her future husband. They married three years later. A year after that she became a Christian. In the first few years, they had bumps along the way, just as many marriages do. MarLo sometimes struggled as she compared her marriage to others. At times, she honestly wondered if she had made a mistake. But she knew one thing. They were committed to working through their issues to make their marriage strong.

Twelve years into the ups and downs, they finally had a breakthrough. While in counseling, they were able to see how the multiple marriages of their parents (his mom's third, her mom's fifth, and both dads remarried) left them with a faulty assumption that all marriages eventually dissolve.

She vividly remembers the day when the counselor explained that they both lived every day as if the other shoe was about to drop. That statement resonated. It also challenged MarLo to stop worrying about the end of her marriage and to work on the day-to-day of their relationship.

Two years after that breakthrough counseling session, she gave birth to their only daughter. MarLo says, "She was a living reminder to us of God's restoration and healing in our marriage. I adored our little family."

Now That's a Happily Ever After, Right?

Many of you might stumble over stories with a "happily ever after" because you are making it day by day. You have not received the miracle yet. You love Jesus with all of your heart, but it's hard when others have it easier or they don't understand your situation. Or perhaps you started with a happily ever after and it changed over time.

The summer after her daughter turned seven, MarLo's husband came down with what they believed to be a severe case of the flu. Days of illness turned into weeks. Doctors tried but failed to find out what was wrong.

Her husband began to exhibit periods of high anxiety and paranoia, constantly asking where she had been, who she was with and what she was doing. One night, they talked into the early morning hours, crying together as they attempted to understand what was happening.

That night, MarLo says that she saw herself and her husband as if from a distance. "I saw a broken little boy and a broken little girl that God had brought together." Her love and resolve deepened. She would hang on to that love weeks later when her husband spiraled into depression. It took two hospitalizations, a month of treatments and medications to alleviate the symptoms. Shortly thereafter he lost his job where he had worked for 10 years as a computer programmer.

MarLo was now the sole wage earner for her family. In almost every sense, she had lost the husband she once had. He wasn't able to work. He struggled with simple household tasks. She moved from wife to caregiver. This wasn't what she had in mind for her marriage or her life. In fact, it was the direct opposite.

Several people, including her counselor, advised her that it was all too much and she should leave. They assured her that everyone would understand.

Their words only made her angry. She didn't have the husband she once had, but she vowed to be with him as he battled this sickness. She didn't deny that she was sad, or even angry, at the sickness and sometimes at him, but she wanted others to know that she was in a real marriage, hardships and all.

FORGIVING WHEN THINGS CHANGE FOR THE WORSE

I have met MarLo many times at different events. She's a beautiful brunette with a breathtaking smile. She is one of those personalities that draw people to her because she's engaging, fun and filled with life. I had no idea of her struggles with her marriage until a conversation a couple of years back. From the outside looking in, a stranger wouldn't know her daily personal battle. When she does share her story, she is completely honest about the hardships; but as she says, she is also "hope-filled."

Not long ago, I shared MarLo's story with my husband. We walk two or three miles each evening, and it's when we have our deepest conversations. After telling her story, my husband reminded me of the time when I was sick. At 32, I was diagnosed with aggressive breast cancer that spread to my lymph nodes. I was a young mom to three, and Richard and I had been married for only 12 years. As I went through chemo, radiation and three surgeries, my husband felt helpless. He couldn't fix me. He couldn't make things better. He could only love me through it.

When I was going through chemo, I noticed hair in the shower one morning, and more in the sink. That made sense. Except that the hair wasn't mine. Somehow I kept my long brown hair through weeks of intense chemo while my husband lost much of his over the next year. It was total stress. It was the fear of the unknown and our battle for me to get well. To this day, I believe that Richard lost his hair 20 years before he was supposed to.

As we walked, Richard confided how my sickness had affected him. "You have to face the loss of normalcy every day," he said, "not just of what you had, but the loss of what you might not ever have again."

That's when I realized what he was saying. MarLo wasn't struggling to forgive a sick husband. She was trying to forgive what she had lost.

No one ever advised my husband to leave me when I was sick. It would have been inconceivable. This is where MarLo and my husband's story intersect yet are markedly different. Each chose to love his or her spouse through illness. Each experienced good days and bad days. Each battled uncertainty, hospital visits and scary diagnoses.

But Richard and I received our happily ever after. Twenty years later, cancer and hospital visits are a dim memory for us.

Not so for MarLo. Her marriage resembles a bungee cord. At times it has been nearly normal. For a season her husband turned a corner. He was doing more around the house. He picked up their daughter after school every day. He started crafting beautiful pens that were a work of art. He began to dream again, talking about becoming a motorcycle mechanic, working on the Harley-Davidson motorcycles he enjoyed. He even enrolled in school.

For the first time in years he began to take care of himself, pay his own bills, get up on a regular schedule and make new friends. He was fully living, enjoying school and maintaining As, and talking about work once school was complete.

It felt good to be dreaming together again.

In the spring of 2012, her husband had a motorcycle accident and suffered a brain injury, several broken ribs and a broken foot requiring surgery. MarLo spent a week with her husband in the hospital and brought him home to recover. Later, doctors informed her that the combination of the brain injury and being off of his meds for several days had put her husband in a worse place than before.

Suddenly all the ground gained was taken away.

She was left once again to wonder if she would ever have a normal marriage relationship or a normal life.

ANOTHER WHO HASN'T RECEIVED HER HAPPILY EVER AFTER

Shannon was raised by an addicted, mentally ill mother.[1] Like MarLo, Shannon is a strong, faith-filled woman; and again, from the outside looking in, you'd never guess her story.

Shannon recalls how as a young girl things were emotionally turbulent night and day. She once traveled by ambulance, listening as her mother begged for death to take her. Another time she stood at the door as social workers, flanked by police, tried to take her and her siblings into foster care. It wasn't unusual for Shannon to sit on her mom so that she wouldn't run onto the busy highway.

It was not a life for a young girl.

When the house was quiet, Shannon pulled out her Bible and, as she describes it, "tucked herself close in with Jesus." She longed for those moments, knowing that in His presence she could offer up the bad parts of her day.

In exchange, her young heart felt free.

When asked how such a young girl could know to seek out God, she said that her mom took all of the kids to church when they were young. To Shannon, church was truly a sanctuary—a safe place. She experienced peace there. She carved out that same peace in her chaotic, troubled home.

Eventually, Shannon grew up and left to marry a good man she loved. She had babies and she created a safe environment where they would thrive, and they did.

For several years, her mother lived separately from her, but the day came when it appeared that Shannon's mother could not take care of herself physically or mentally. If left alone, she might not survive. After prayer and talking with her family, Shannon asked her mother to move in.

Wouldn't it be nice if such a sacrificial act had a happy ending? It doesn't. After several years, it's still hard.

Every day.

Though her mother is no longer an addict, she is far from whole. Shannon says that her relationship with her mother drives her to a place of strength. She realizes that not everyone would invite her mother in under these circumstances, but for her it was a personal and family decision. She also states that she could not do this on her own. "If I don't give Him my burdens every morning, it gets too heavy for me," she says. "I am still desperate for God's Word. I still receive the same results as I did when I was just a girl. It offers freedom and peace that passes all understanding. Even on the hardest days."

Both MarLo and Shannon made a conscious choice to live and love through an unchanging situation.

They are not alone.

YOUR UNCHANGING SITUATION

Perhaps your unchanging situation looks nothing like MarLo's or Shannon's, but you relate. There are thousands of situations that seem unchanging, even as people try to do the right thing.

Situations like when you've been fighting to keep a marriage together, but it's not there yet. Or you've been mired in debt as unexpected circumstances or economic downturns keep you swimming upstream just to stay afloat. Or when you marry a great guy only to inherit a mother-in-law who is unkind and unable or unwilling to see the harm it inflicts on you and your marriage. You *could* alter these situations, but only by taking yourself out of them, and that's not an option for you.

Shannon knew in advance that taking in her mother wasn't an easy choice. "It's a decision I made with prayer," she says, "but only with the knowledge that I'm not strong enough on my own to carry another person's pain." She loves and forgives her mother daily, but only with the covering, the comfort, the hope and the daily supernatural strength found in Christ.

FORGIVING AGAIN AND AGAIN

In Matthew 18:21-35, when Peter approached Jesus about how to forgive, he asked, "How often should I forgive someone who sins against me? Seven times seven?" (v. 21, *NLT*). (Some scholars believe he is stating seven times in a lifetime from the same person.)

Jesus responds, "No, not seven times . . .but seventy times seven" (v. 22, *NLT*).

Four hundred and ninety? One. Two. Three. Four-hundred-and-eighty-seven to go!

The word "forgive" in this story refers to *Aphiemi* forgiveness (described in chapter 2). Jesus was asking Peter to negate the thought that we forgive a brother a limited number of times in a lifetime. To further define His point, He shared a parable:

A king brings his accounts up to date and discovers that some of his servants borrowed money and didn't pay it back. Some ignored the debt, and as time lapsed, interest and penalties accumulated. One unlucky guy was brought in. His debt was 10,000 talents, a sum equal to over a million dollars in today's currency. It was such a massive debt that he wouldn't be able to pay it in a lifetime.

The king orders the man to be sold to pay his debt, but also that his children and his wife and everything he owns be put up for sale as well. The man falls to his face and begs for mercy. "I will pay it all," he says.

Everyone in the room knows it's a desperate promise that can never be fulfilled. However, the king is moved by the man's plight, and in an unexpected decision he releases him and forgives his debt.

What would you or I do? Perhaps we would hit the streets with a dance in our step and run for home with the good news! Not this man. He leaves the king and goes straight to a fellow servant who owes him 10 talents—one thousandth of what the king had just pardoned—and demands payment. He grabs the servant by the throat as the servant falls to his knees and begs for mercy. To no avail. The man calls for his arrest and he is thrown in prison.

Unfortunately, other servants saw this. They all worked together. They knew what their fellow servant had just received from the king, and the gossip around the courtyard was, "How could he do this when his massive debt was forgiven by the king?"

Several of them run straight to the throne and tell the king what they saw.

The king calls in the man. "You evil servant! I forgave you that tremendous debt. . . . Shouldn't you have mercy on your fellow servant, just as I had mercy on you?" (vv. 32-33, *NLT*). The king retracts his offer and the man is sent to prison until he can pay his entire debt.

When the parable ends, Jesus looks at Peter and says, "That's what my heavenly Father will do to you if you refuse to forgive your brothers and sisters from your heart" (v. 35, *NLT*).

The man in the parable overlooked the kindness and benevolence of the king who gave him a gift he could never purchase on his own.

But not MarLo and Shannon. And not you. You have chosen the harder road of mercy. You are completely aware that you may never receive a happily ever after, at least defined by others. You have far exceeded 490 acts of forgiveness. You don't debate about how much or at what point forgiveness is no longer deserved.

MarLo and Shannon aren't martyrs, and while they are not unmarked by their struggles, they are not identified by them either. They purposely have chosen to forgive the lack of their happily ever after, but only as they seek out what God can give in such a hard place.

Peter was asking how many times he should forgive; but Jesus led him to a much more loving question: How will you handle the mercy I have poured out on you?

> **οὕτως** [Greek] translated *houtos:* (1) in this way; (2) in this manner.

THE UNEQUAL ROAD TO FORGIVENESS

Paul instructs us in Colossians 3:12 that as God's chosen, dearly and loved, to clothe ourselves with compassion, kindness, humility, gentleness and patience. Much like we get up and dress every day for the elements and the occasion, we are taught to put on those traits that will reflect God's love in us no matter the day or the circumstances in which we find ourselves.

But the instructions continue: "Bear with each other and forgive one another if any of you has a grievance against someone. Forgive as the Lord forgave you. And over all these virtues put on love, which binds them all together in perfect unity" (vv. 13-14).

The first emphasis on forgiveness in this teaching is *charizomai*. As you "bear with one another" or put up with each other, you love generously. You show mercy. As it shifts to *houtos* forgive it takes on a very different definition. It means that you are to act or respond in a certain way.

"Forgive how?" Peter asked.

Forgive as the Lord forgave you.

As you *houtos* forgive, you choose daily, hourly, over and over again to love in a certain way, and it can be one of the most difficult choices a person can make. Others might not understand, so your support system may be lacking. Sometimes it can appear that your prayers are unheard. Can we admit how discouraging that can sometimes be?

If MarLo or Shannon or you were the main character in the parable told by Jesus, the story would look vastly different. Let's take a second look.

A woman walks out of the presence of the king who just forgave a massive debt. She dances out of his presence with joy; and as she crosses the street, she runs into a fellow sufferer who also has a debt against her.

She could imprison him. She could lash out. But somehow this woman forgives, but only out of the abundance of mercy she has just received.

She is filled with awe over what the king gave her.

The fellow sufferer who walks beside her may or may not be aware of the gift that he has just received.

Her love for this fellow servant is demonstrating exactly what Jesus was trying to show Peter when answering the tougher questions, like, "How many times am I supposed to forgive?" For that day and that moment she is clothed with mercy, gentleness and patience. Not out of her own strength, but out of what God has already held up as an offering to her.

The circumstances are very, very real, but so is God.

Climb In

When I was teetering on the edge of my teen years, I often climbed up the wide branches of a Mimosa tree splashed with pink buds into a crudely fashioned tree house. In that safe place I read books. I thought big thoughts. It was a sanctuary built out of planks and throwaway wood, but it was heaven to me as chaos raged inside my small home on Latimer Street.

When I became a believer, nothing at home changed. Not one single thing. It was just as hard as the day before I believed in Christ, except everything began to change inside of me. My second safe place became a small altar at church. There were many times when I knelt in that little church, and no one had a clue why I wept.

I cried because things were hard and I wasn't wise enough or old enough to change a thing about my family or the way it made me feel. But God knew.

The more I grew in my faith and aged chronologically, the more I realized what I was being given in those precious one-on-one times with God. When I shut out the world in my safe place, I shut myself in with God. I tapped in to His love for me, which led me to love others. I held out my hands like a beggar and He poured out peace that was beyond my situation. I grew to understand what a selfless, rich gift I had been given through the cross. That led me to want others to have that same understanding.

Even those I both loved and sometimes hated at the same time.

The Source

In order to offer up mercy daily, it cannot take place without going to the resource from which it flows. It's something Shannon incredibly grasped as a young girl with no one to show her how or why, but the Holy Spirit covered a little girl in a hard place and clothed her with His love and she gained strength.

For most of us, we know we are to forgive, but we try to do it on our own and at some point we just run out of mercy or patience or even love.

In Exodus 33, we read that Moses daily walked into a place of prayer. He was surrounded by bickering, unhappy, grumbling, contrary people. Thousands of them. And for a number of years. His situation was unchanging, even as He held tightly to promises that things would get better one day. He could have thrown his hands up in the air and said, "I quit!" Instead he sat quietly in that tent every day. In awe, those outside the tent watched a cloud of glory descend. Something miraculous took place in that tent.

When God asked Moses to build the tent, it wasn't because He needed a place to live. He instructed Moses to build a specific place where fellowship between Himself and Moses could occur. Moses was astute enough that he marched into that quiet, shut-off place every day while people and life hammered on outside (see Exod. 33:7-11).

If you are *houtos* forgiving every day—loving a person beyond his or her lovability, there is a safe place for you where God invites you to be clothed in His mercy and strength. It's not hiding in isolation or pretending that your circumstances don't exist. It's freely walking into a nurturing environment and the shelter from an ongoing storm.

Psalm 91:4 describes that shelter as a place where God covers with "his feathers" and "will shelter you with his wings" (*NLT*).

We were never expected to live out our faith as a solitary adventure, but to receive relationship and the benefits of being His child, and all that comes with it. Even in the hard places.

Especially in the hard places.

Perhaps like MarLo and Shannon, you are forgiving daily, but you feel exposed rather than covered. Maybe you've been trying to grit your teeth and power your way through it without His help.

Are you willing to climb into that safe place today? Perhaps your happily ever after will come one day. Shannon and MarLo both believe theirs will come; but until that time, they—and you—are called to find what is needed in a God who treasures you and waits daily for communion so that He can pour out the daily manna you need.

Just You and God

1. In what ways are you forgiving daily?

_____

_____

_____

_____

2. Read Psalm 91:1-2. Rewrite this with your name inserted. Make it your prayer for today.

_____

_____

_____

_____

3. What do you wish others understood about your situation or your choice to forgive? In light of Jesus' words to Peter, what do you believe Christ would say to you about your choice?

_____

_____

_____

_____

4. If you are covered or clothed with His mercy, what might that look like today?

_____

_____

_____

_____

5. Do you ever feel like you try to "gut it out"? Why or why not? What is one thing you can do differently?

_____

_____

_____

_____

_____

6. Read Ephesians 1:15-20; 3:16-20. What do you need from what Jesus is offering to you? Answer in the form of a prayer. Place this prayer somewhere where you can read it daily.

_____

_____

_____

_____

_____

HOUTOS PRINCIPLE

You pour out mercy out of the abundance you receive.

TO *HOUTOS* FORGIVE

Create a sanctuary and climb in daily.

PRAYER

Dear Jesus, Cover me. Overwhelm me with Your strength. Give me what I need for today, and tomorrow we'll meet again.

Note
1. Not her real name.

Suzanne Eller

9

You Get Over the Little Stuff

*All of us are human and humans sometimes do and say things that
are demeaning to other people.*

Gary D. Chapman, *Things I Wish I'd Known Before We Got Married*

You've made it this far, and you wipe your forehead in relief. You picked up this book because you wanted to let the little stuff go, and suddenly that seems insignificant in the light of Stephanie's or Carlie's or Karen's stories.

However, the little stuff is just as important. Did you know that there are 157 references to forgiveness in 129 verses in the *New International Version* of the Bible? Forgiveness is a topic that Jesus talked about often.

He understood human nature.

He also witnessed the petty arguments, like the time when John and James, two brothers, quarreled over who was going to sit by Jesus in heaven (see Mark 10:35-45). Kind of reminds me of the times when my kids ran out door shouting, "Shotgun!" As a weary mom, I often wondered why that was such a big deal. Why would they tussle over where to sit? Perhaps Jesus felt the same. Like a parent, He set them straight when they bickered among themselves.

No, guys. I don't pick James, John, and Peter to do all the cool stuff.

Didn't you just see Me feed 5,000 with one boy's lunch? Why are you worrying so?

Peter, yes, you really messed up, but your mistakes are not greater than My plan for you.

Everyday concerns caused friction among these men. They had differing personalities and strengths, just like us. They experienced fatigue and close quarters (smelly feet and long road trips), which offered multiple opportunities to get on each other's nerves and build up resentment. Any one of these everyday issues had the potential to divide friendships, scatter a ministry or create confusion and hurt feelings among friends.

Little things do matter.

That's Mine, Let Me Have It

In the mornings, I drive to a local university library and settle in to a small, cramped nook under a stairwell. It has a worn leather couch and a window that looks out over a small outdoor area where a lone squirrel plays. It's tucked away, like a comfy cave.

As I wrote this book, I sat in that comforting place. Suddenly, I sensed God asking me to take my fingers off the keyboard and listen.

Have you offered up every area of unforgiveness, Suzie?

When you write a book on a challenging topic like forgiveness, the Holy Spirit often slips in to examine your heart. I wasn't surprised by it, but I was surprised by what He showed me.

Several years ago, a drunk driver hit my teenage son head-on. The driver died on impact. The wreck left my son and another boy severely injured; a third boy sustained minor injuries. This drunk-driving incident slammed into not only my son's life, but into ours as well. The financial aftereffects threaded through our family for years because the driver was underinsured. My son lay in a hospital bed for 37 days and came home in a wheelchair. After a year of intense physical therapy he moved from the wheelchair to a cane, and eventually he recovered. In fact, today he is an avid runner and has completed three marathons and numerous half-marathons.

When our son was hurt, we were so grateful that he had survived, and so immersed in battling insurance and overwhelming medical bills that we had no time to process our feelings. We were asked numerous times why we didn't pursue litigation. At that time, the legal advice was to take his wife to court, but we couldn't do it. It wasn't her fault that her husband drank too much.

Time passed. Memories and feelings that came along with the wreck got buried. After all, I had my son. How could I be angry?

As I sat in that quiet place, I felt my precious Savior asking me to take a second look at the unresolved, buried hurt that lingered.

Will you give Me that, Suzie?

I wrote these words in my journal that day:

Today, I choose to forgive the man who hurt my son because he was drunk and climbed in a car. I let go of the hurt over my son's injuries and the helplessness I felt sitting at his bedside night and day for six weeks.

I let go of the resentment over the bills we were left to pay, over our dreams delayed or taken away because of those bills. Today, I forgive willingly and thank God for His grace and provision during that time, for people who blanketed us with love, for a church and family and friends that filled in the gaps as we tried to make it day by day emotionally. Today, I let go.

The Holy Spirit reminded me that the words in this book are not just words for you. They are for me too. When I live a forgiving lifestyle, I open the door to His presence in the areas that have been wounded. My tears fell as I sensed His peace settle in that old wound.

Now that's big stuff, Suzie.

You're right. You see, God wasn't through speaking; He showed me more. Small things. Annoyances. Things I held onto without realizing it.

One was a comment made by someone a long time ago. I had just started speaking on a regular basis. My children were on their way out of the nest, and the timing was perfect. I was traveling once a month out of state. At a gathering, I was excitedly talking about an upcoming conference when someone stated, "You must not love your husband very much."

I didn't know how to respond. Of course, I love my husband.

After an awkward pause, I tried to explain that together we prayerfully considered every event, and Richard was my biggest cheerleader. My husband delighted in the fact that I shared the gospel. I further explained that family and home were my first priority and always had been, and that if I had chosen to work outside the home rather than full-time ministry, I would be gone far more than one weekend a month.

The more I tried to explain the more she shook her head. "Sorry, Charlie," she said. "That's how I see it."

The reason I debated this for so long with her wasn't that I was trying to do the right thing, but that I wanted her to see it from my vantage point. It was also because this person's opinion carried weight. She was a caring person, and to be honest, her words blindsided me and made me angry.

To pursue this conversation would only ruin a special celebration, so eventually I shut up, but only verbally. Her words played out in my head the rest of the day, the rest of the week and a hundred times over the next few months.

This is where offense can fester. It's in the playground of our mind. It's where we rehearse what we should have said, what we wished we had said and how triumphant we feel in that pretend moment when they realize their wrong and repent. As I mentally went over and over that conversation, the angrier and the more justified I felt. Believe me, I didn't hold my tongue in those pretend conversations. I showed her the error of her ways. Each time, I made her feel shame at how she had made me feel.

One day, I was engaged in that playground when I felt God asking me to stop. May I be completely truthful? It wasn't easy. Each time I started to go there—to make myself feel taller, bigger, better than that person—I felt convicted. Each time I admitted that it wasn't a place God wanted me to linger, and I stopped. That doesn't mean I wasn't tempted to go back, even five minutes later; but to do so was to be disobedient to what I knew God was speaking.

Eventually, if you put down something long enough and often enough, you recognize it for what it is and the damage it can do, and it's no longer a temptation. Over time, that is what took place, and I went on with life.

So why was the Holy Spirit bringing this to light now?

God revealed unresolved feelings. There was a polite barrier in place. When I thought about that moment, it still felt bad; and most importantly, though she might not even remember the conversation, I still had a desire to set the record straight.

For some reason that day, one person said something insensitive. It was one negative comment among a thousand positive ones. The broader picture is that she saw things differently than I did because she was older and, in her day, women didn't travel away from family for any reason. As old-fashioned as that may have felt to me, she saw it through her own lens, and she's entitled to her opinion.

I was entitled to take it personally and remain offended, or see it in context and move on. I could focus on the 999 other things this person said that were positive and offer grace for the 1. And while I was at it, I could take a look at all of the times I had said something I wish I hadn't and be grateful for the grace *I* had received.

This allowed me to rest in what I knew to be true. I fully grasped my husband's support and excitement about what I do. Why in the world had I invested so much energy and thought to this? As the Holy Spirit peeled away the layers, I realized it was less her words that hurt and more my lack of confidence at the time. Those words shouldn't have held power. They only gained power as I took those words and soaked in them, fed the hurt and allowed them to fester and grow deep roots.

Funny how we can hang on to one slip of the tongue for so long. In some ways, it might even be easier to forgive big things. They are so huge we can't help but see them. But we often fail to understand how little things compiled are just as large or larger.

Are you willing to ask God to shine a light into the recessed corners of your heart? I don't know what He will show you; that's between you and God. The end result is always to draw you closer to Him.

WE ALL HAVE ISSUES

Letting go of the small stuff means that we take our eyes off of everybody else to look at our own issues. Jesus said, "And why worry about a speck in your friend's eye when you have a log in your own?

How can you think of saying to your friend, 'Let me help you get rid of that speck in your eye,' when you can't see past the log in your own eye?" (Matt. 7:3-4. *NLT*).

I've confessed a lot in this chapter. Unfortunately, there's more.

I get annoyed when someone raises his or her voice to make a point.

I struggle when people are rude or use their power to make others feel small.

I slow down in traffic when someone is tailing my bumper.

If I think you are bullying me, I'll push back in a heartbeat.

If I want to look at the root of these, it probably goes back to when I was a young girl who felt helpless in a dysfunctional home. I draw a tight line at what I perceive to be aggressive behavior. This *can* be a good thing, but it can also mean that I take offense easily in these areas. I can perceive that someone is a bully or aggressive when he or she is just trying to state his or her opinion. I can get overly sensitive and take on the conversation or behavior police role when it's not needed.

We all have issues. Have you taken time to note yours?

Don't feel alone as you so identify them. Nothing is new. Paul and Barnabas had a disagreement so sharp that they parted ways for a time (see Acts 15:36-41). Martha was so irked at her sister Mary that she went to Jesus to tattle (see Luke 10:38-42).

Even the most extraordinary people in the Bible had issues.

We have opportunities every day to overreact, hold grudges, distance ourselves from an annoying person or put on a mask that says everything is okay when it's not. Forgiving the small stuff is important because it is your day-to-day experiences that propel you forward or keep you stuck. They affect your heart, which affects your attitude, which affects your relationships, even your relationship with God.

Because we are human, we are going to encounter offense or create offense.

Sometimes it might be someone else's fault, but what if it is your issue rising up? When you look at your own issues in an offense, it's admitting that God is still working on you, performing the in-depth, transforming work of renewing your mind so that you can know what God's will is (see Rom. 12:2). It offers insight. You come clean about the things that trip your trigger, and why.

When I get offended over something small, I ask, "Is this a true offense or did it just set off my emotions because I'm still a work in progress in this area?"

If it's my issue, that question allows me to respond in the appropriate way.

That means, when someone is tailing me in traffic, I don't slow down and force him to drive in the correct manner (my way). I simply move into the passing lane. If he or she wants to drive recklessly, I don't have to respond recklessly.

If someone raises her voice, I don't have to raise mine. If I disagree with someone or she disagrees with me, I can admit—in this vast world of people with different experiences, backgrounds and cultures—that there are going to be differing opinions. If someone loves to debate, I don't have to engage or try to convince him or her to think like I do.

Perhaps you've been pointing at everyone else. Is it possible that you have issues God is still working on? (We all do.) Is it conceivable that because of the past, there's a raw area that causes you to be super-sensitive? If it's your issue, you are free to offer it to God one more time, to apologize to those you love and to relate to people or that situation in the proper context.

WHEN YOUR ISSUES CREATE PROBLEMS

Because I'm in ministry, I often ride with strangers. I once climbed into a car with a really nice couple to go to a restaurant. The man took the wheel, the wife sat in the front seat. When the man turned the key, he changed. He rocketed out of the parking lot and nearly collided with another car. He jammed the horn and called the person an idiot under his breath. I held on to the back of the seat and double-checked my safety belt. It was a horrific drive.

If a car ahead of him was in the passing lane and not going as fast as he was (far above the speed limit), his face grew red and he pushed as close as he could until the other car moved over to the other lane. If the car didn't move because of traffic, he commented that they "shouldn't have been in this lane anyway."

I was not only uncomfortable with what was taking place, but I also felt endangered. And I felt bad for his wife. Her fingers clutched the door handle; and when she glanced back, the look on her face was one of helpless embarrassment. When that car ride finally ended (the longest 15 minutes I'd ever endured), I jumped out. I made sure that I didn't ride with that person for the rest of the day.

It wasn't just that it was risky; it made no sense. Several people were endangered in that short distance. What if there had been a baby tucked away in a car seat in the backseat of one of the cars he nearly sideswiped? What if his aggressive driving or the sight of a grown man waving his arms wildly caused an elderly driver to panic?

His wife later apologized when we were alone. "He turns into a monster when he drives," she said. "I really hate getting in the car with him. I've talked to him and tried to explain. My kids won't get in the car with him at all."

If you were to ask this man why he acted that way, he would possibly point out the things he had witnessed in others: drivers who remained in the passing lane; people who drove too slowly; stupid drivers. The list could go on.

But the real offense in this instance was his.

Now this is the hard part. You've probably agreed with every word until this moment. Now let's shift the spotlight. Has someone you loved pointed out an offense more than once? Are there times when your anger or behavior escalates and you push on regardless of how it makes others feel? Do you justify your behavior?

Don't discount what God is trying to do in you.

Some might say this man was a confident driver, or just an aggressive driver; but selfishness was the foundational problem. He was insensitive to his wife's feelings. He dismissed loved ones who said it made them feel unsafe. He didn't take into consideration what might happen if he caused an accident, or how saving five minutes would seem ridiculous if a child or any other person was killed or injured.

The symptoms showed up in his driving, but the problem was that he couldn't see his own offenses and how they affected his relationships, because his focus was on everyone else's faults and how they made him feel. There's no way I could see behind the scenes of his family dynamics, but the look on his wife's face and her whispered confession that his grown children refused to get in the car revealed deeper problems in this man's relationships than poor driving.

When we listen to trusted loved ones who have our best interests at heart, we start to climb over mountains that have stood in the way of answered prayer.

Father, fix this.

I don't like that there is such disharmony in my family.

I don't know why everyone is so upset with me all the time.

If this man had paused to really hear what was being said, his blood pressure might have stabilized rather than skyrocketed every time he got behind the wheel of a car. But most importantly, it could be the tool he needed to address the core issues that God wanted to heal.

In Irvin D. Yalom's book *The Gift of Therapy*, a time-tested book for counselors and therapists, Dr. Yalom says, "There comes a time when attention must be paid to the patient's own role in the sequence of events." He goes on to say that "even if the things that happen to you is someone else's fault, I want to look at the other 1 percent—the part that is your responsibility. We have to look at your role, even if it's very limited, because that's where I can be the most help."[1]

Dr. Yalom encourages that this type of self-discovery teaches how your behavior is seen by others, how your behavior makes others feel, how it shapes the way people see you and how those three steps combined shape the way you feel about yourself.[2]

It's not easy to look at our own issues. But if it's something that has you tangled and bound, and it's affecting those you love, start listening so that you can be honest about what's holding you back.

Do we listen to everyone? No. If a friend is failing miserably in marriage and offering you advice in your relationship with your spouse, it would be worse than unwise to listen to her. If the motive behind a person's words is to shame you, demean you, belittle you or paint you into a corner, then it's not likely the person has your best interests at heart.

But, there is wisdom in listening to those who have prayed with you, who do have your best interests at heart, who are courageous enough to have the harder conversations and who love you right where you are.

> ἀγαπάω translated *agapaō* [Greek]: (1) to love; (2) to show love.

WE FORGIVE SO WE CAN LOVE

In John 15, Jesus drew the disciples close. "Love each other," He said. "This is my command. Love each other as I have loved you" (see vv. 12,17).

Why a commandment?

Jesus didn't easily drop commandments. We see them a lot in the Old Testament, but we see them rarely in the New Testament and always spoken by Jesus in relationship to loving each other or loving God.

Forgiving the big things demonstrates God's love and power in and through us because people can't imagine doing it without His help. But in the everyday, in the mundane, that's where God shows up as we intentionally love as Christ loved us. He shows up when we could handle it ourselves, in our own way, but we choose His way instead.

His way looks nothing like ours.

How many times do we choose to hold a grudge instead of to forgive?

How many times do we gossip about someone instead of giving her grace?

How many times do we say those things that we know pierce the heart of a person because we are angry or tired or frustrated, or just plain ol' irritated? Especially with the people we love the best. They are the easiest to treat disrespectfully, because they love us. They'll accept our apology, right?

This isn't about condemnation; it's about transformation.

When forgiveness becomes a way of living, it shows up in your words. It shows up in your behavior. It is woven in your character. People know whether they can trust you. It's not that you live without giving or taking offense, but that you handle it in such a way that God's love begins to be revealed through you.

Love each other as I have loved you.

The word found in John 15:12 is *agapaō*. It's similar to a familiar Greek word, *agape*, which mean's God's unconditional love; but *agapaō* shifts the focus from His love for us to His love *in* us. It takes place when God is so evident in you that others can't help but be drawn to Him.

Years ago, when I discovered this word, I was so excited! This became a prayer.

Perhaps you have met that person who just exudes God. They are down to earth and live a real life, but you see Jesus in them. You walk away and say, "That's what I want!"

I wanted that in my own life.

WHY IT MATTERS

Years ago, I went to church with a man I highly respected. Then I went to work with him for a short time. His moral standards were high. He was a hard worker. He didn't arrive late. He was a man of integrity. But he was also easily offended.

At church, he was lighthearted; but at work, his quills were on point, ready to shoot. It wasn't one day or one moment, but many days and lots of moments. Thirty years have passed since that time, and as I look back, I wonder if perhaps he hated his job. Perhaps something happened that made him distrustful of others. Something was going on that changed his demeanor at work. My heart wasn't to judge him, but to learn from his example.

The problem with living easily offended is that if you had asked his co-workers if he was a moral man, they would have responded with an overwhelming yes. But if asked if he showed the love of Christ, sadly, the answer would have been a firm no.

Agapaō love reaches beyond offense to display a message of love to our families, within in our churches and communities and even to strangers and acquaintances. It's not perfection. I don't have to be Suzie Sunshine or pretend that I am always joy-filled; but it does mean that I am to love difficult people. *Agapaō* love means responding kindly when you feel frazzled and have waited in line for 30 minutes. It's loving the neighbor who decides to mow his lawn at 7 AM on a Saturday morning. It's a genuine apology when you say something hurtful to your son or daughter. Jesus loves us even in those times when we fall way short. In response, we "love the Lord your God with all your heart and with all your soul and with all your mind" and "love your neighbor as yourself" (Matt. 22:37-39).

It's intentional in the beginning. Are you tired of that word yet? We live deliberate lives of kindness, gentleness, self-control, until it becomes a natural response.

BUT HOW DO YOU DO IT?

My dad who raised me but isn't my biological dad share the same laugh. When I get super tickled, I laugh so hard it sounds wheezy. We call it my Mutley laugh. Attractive image, I know. But when I laugh like that, my sister will point out, "You sound just like Dad!"

It's revealing, isn't it? We don't share any DNA, but because he was there from the time I was nine months old all the way through to today, I bear some resemblance to him in mannerisms.

If you want to love like Jesus, it will come through knowing Him and being identified as His. If a stranger asks who my father is, I don't respond with the words, "Well, he's my dad, but not necessarily my bio dad, but I've been his daughter since I was . . ." I don't go there, even when people point out our differences (he's small, I'm tall). It's with an inner confidence that I say Jim Morrison is my father.

Knowing someone or something comes through devotion.

Have you ever read how God worked through the disciples and thought, *I want that, too!* In the book of Acts, we read that these men have regrouped. Remember, they were once in hiding and afraid. Now they are anything but. In Acts 2:42, we find them devoted to teaching, to fellowship with each other, and to prayer. But it is in verse 43 that we see the results of that devotion. A deep sense of awe has come over them at what God is doing in them and through them.

To be devoted is to be dedicated, committed and constant in something. My beautiful mom is devoted to cleanliness. She can be sick and struggling to breathe while digging out a closet one more time to make sure no extra clutter has managed to sneak in. No weeds are allowed in her garden. No loads of laundry ever rest in a chair. My childhood memories will always be intermingled with the smell of pine-scented cleaner.

We can be devoted to our favorite television programs, never missing a show as we faithfully watch or DVR, and celebrate our favorite characters. We can be devoted to a cause, a sport, a hobby or to health or appearance. A friend of mine will always be known as a Sooner fan because of his Sooner flag, Sooner T-shirt, Sooner season tickets and his Sooner enthusiasm.

To be devoted to my Savior is to pursue Him and my relationship with Him. It's a theme that continues to crop up as we discuss what it is to forgive. Devotion might look different for each of us. For me, it means that each day there is time carved out just for my relationship with God. I start with a devotion, which leads deeper in the Word, and I journal. That journal is a scattering of prayers, insights from Scripture, honest admissions and joy-filled praise. The journal also contains lists, where I might pause to write down the three items I need to pick up at the grocery store that day, so that I can remove that distraction and go back to my time with Jesus.

Devotion, for me, is pausing in the middle of the day to breathe thanks when I see or experience something beautiful; or it's driving down the road, my heart heavy because it's been a really hard day, and I invite Him into those feelings and that situation.

It's not necessarily a formula but a deliberate choice on your part to live beyond the boundaries of religious tradition.

Just You and God

1. When the little stuff gets ignored, it becomes the big stuff in your life. What little stuff annoys, irks or is hard to forgive?

   _____

   _____

   _____

   _____

   _____

2. In this chapter, I confessed some issues from the past that have often contributed to conflict in my life. As I described these issues, which of yours came to mind?

   _____

   _____

   _____

   _____

   _____

3. Read 2 Timothy 2:22-23. In verse 22, Paul instructs Timothy to run toward righteous living, faithfulness, love and peace. Describe the ways you can do this in everyday life. Secondly, verse 23 asks us to stay away from foolish arguments. Describe what a foolish argument might look like and one thing you can do to walk away from it.

   _____

   _____

   _____

   _____

   _____

4. Describe one constructive criticism a loved one might offer you (or has offered you) in regard to issues that cause you pain.

How do you respond to that advice or constructive criticism? What truth might you find in it?

_____

_____

_____

_____

_____

5. In John 7:37-38, Jesus shouted to the crowds that they were looking for their Source in the wrong places. What did He offer them, and what does this mean to you? How can that Source splash out of you into your marriage, into your relationships with your children or your friends, or in relationships that need healing?

_____

_____

_____

_____

_____

_____

6. What would devotion to Jesus look like for you? What do you hope to gain as you devote yourself to loving Him?

_____

_____

_____

_____

_____

AGAPAŌ PRINCIPLE

Jesus draws others to Himself as His presence is evident in you.

TO AGAPAŌ LOVE

Devote yourself to knowing Jesus.

PRAYER

Jesus, today I want You more than yesterday. Tomorrow I want You more than today. Pour out Your Living Water on my life in such a way that others see You in me. In Your strong and amazing name, amen.

Note

1. Irvin D. Yalom, *The Gift of Therapy* (New York: HarperCollins Publishers, 2002), pp. 139-140.

1 0

You Exchange Your Anger for His

*I knew that my heart and mind would always be tempted to feel anger—
to find blame and hate. But I resolved that when the negative feelings
came upon me, I wouldn't wait for them to grow or fester. I would always
turn immediately to the Source of all true power: I would turn to God
and let His love and forgiveness protect and save me.*

Immaculee Ilibagiza, *Left to Tell: Discovering God Amidst the Rwandan Holocaust*

There's no such thing as evil.

I've been told that.

Oh, really?

In her book *Undaunted*, Christine Caine sits with 14 young
women in Greece, just outside the Thessaloniki shipping port. She
is surrounded by girls from Ukraine, Bulgaria, Georgia, Albania,
Romania, Russia, Uzbekistan and Nigeria—all recently rescued
from sex trafficking. The youngest is 16, the oldest 18.

They had been lured by promises of a better life, with slick
brochures and meetings with agents that provided details of opportunities in Greece. These girls are from impoverished backgrounds. Their families helped raise money for passage to Greece
to pursue a brighter future, and that left many of them destitute
but hopeful that their sacrifice would benefit their daughters and,
perhaps later on, the family.

When the girls disembarked in Greece, a professionally dressed
woman met them and delivered them to a hotel room. As each girl
unpacked in her room, several men would rush in and begin to beat
and repeatedly rape them. The next day, they began their new life
as moneymaking pawns in the sex and human trafficking industry.

These young girls are representative of thousands sold around the world. They are raped sometimes up to 25 times per day.

As Christine interviewed the girls, one girl named Nadia shared how she and 59 others were forced into a crate. Half of the girls died in the passage from their home country to Greece. Nadia jumped from a two-story building to flee her captors after months of rape and beatings. She miraculously survived and led police back to the house to free the remaining girls.[1]

If you think this is a remote problem, one estimate is that as many as 100,000 girls are trafficked as sex slaves within the United States each year.[2] In my home state, major Interstates serve the trucking industry. In 2011, authorities began to focus on truck stops, where it is known that teens, some as young as 14, often climb into a truck in the middle of the night to offer sex for pay. These teens are often referred to as "lot lizards."

Authorities discovered that many of these children were trapped in the sex slave trade. They were not there by choice or to make quick money, but forced into the industry. Some were runaways, others kidnapped, but all are victims. This knowledge caused many truckers to rethink the way they viewed these children. One ministry that was created is Trucking Against Traffickers. These truckers began to spread the word that sex trafficking was thriving in the United States, how to recognize it and how to help rescue these victims of the sex slave trade.

There it is. Evil in our own backyard. It's hard to hear, much less to stomach, isn't it?

Human trafficking. Scams designed to rob the elderly of their life savings. Incest. The Holocaust. Rwanda. Mass shootings that take the life of the innocent.

Don't tell me there isn't evil in the world.

EVIL MAKES GOD ANGRY

Author Kay Arthur is one of my spiritual heroes. Once I was at a bookseller's convention in Denver, Colorado. I stood in line to pick up a breakfast tray at a publisher's booth. A hand gently took me by the elbow. "You are sitting with me," a voice said. I turned, and it was Kay Arthur.

The Kay Arthur.

"Yes ma'am," I said. (What would you say?) I followed her to her table.

People flocked around her while we ate. Some asked her to sign a book. Others requested an interview. Many lingered, excited for the opportunity to meet this renowned Bible teacher and author. In the middle of our breakfast, she glanced at my new book resting nearby and picked it up.

"Have you seen Suzanne's book?" she asked those who were standing around us. "You need to talk to her too,"

It was a purely unselfish act as she drew the attention away from herself and toward me.

Kay didn't know me, and to this day I'm not sure why she sought me out, but what I discovered as we ate breakfast together is that she is gracious, straightforward and giving. She asked questions about my ministry and my writing and speaking, and offered advice. She asked about my family and told me about hers. She shared her story, tearing up as she described how God had walked with her through painful times, and how much she owed Him. She listened as I shared my story.

When the breakfast was over, we bid each other good-bye, and I left. I quickly bustled down the vast lobby and found a small bathroom at the far end of the convention center, where no one could find me.

I closed myself in a stall and stood quietly for a moment, then the tears came.

For the past several years I had been a mother and a spiritual mom to many, but until that day I had never known what it was like to have that in my own life. I didn't miss what I didn't have, until that moment. It was a gift as she asked me questions, talked openly and encouraged me spiritually.

Why is this story important for this chapter?

Because Kay's words resonated with my heart when I read in her book *When the Hurt Runs Deep,* "There is a time for anger."[3]

For many years, Kay Arthur has devoted her life to studying the Bible. She's not content with superficial scraps or bite-sized sermons. Those years of study are ingrained within her, and she walks in and out of the spotlight as a woman of deep-rooted faith. So, when I read those words from her book *When the Hurt Runs Deep*, it confirmed what I believed must have been true all along. God is angry at evil. Human sex trafficking evil. Travesty during war evil. Babies ripped from momma's arms evil. Incest perpetrated on an innocent child evil.

LET'S DEFINE EVIL

There are entire books written on the subject of evil, and I won't pretend to be an expert on this subject. But what I do know is that when we lump all evil into one category, it's confusing to the person who is asked to forgive the acts of an evildoer.

Evil occurs where and when sin is manifested in the human experience to thwart God's will, and it is at odds with God's plans and purposes for the world. The majority of the references to evil in the Old Testament are defined as: "to lead into trouble, calamity, disaster, harm."

We see this type of evil in action in the book of Genesis as God's chosen people dance while they hold up worthless idols made from gold jewelry and wood and call them god. This is far from God's plan for them, and far from the promises and love God spoke over the nation of Israel. The Israelites walked away from God's purpose and plan, straight into bondage and, eventually, into a wilderness.

This definition of evil breaks God's heart.

It's the type of evil that leads a person to pour herself into something other than God's sheltering love, like addiction or gluttony. It's when we worship material goods while we let others go hungry. It's when we treat others badly. It's living in a way that is the opposite of God's will and hope for humanity.

We see God's heart in the book of Jeremiah, which reads like a letter between a rebellious, runaway child and her parent as the

Israelites plunge deeper into sin and God declares both His love for the nation and His grief and even anger over their disobedience.

A DEEPER EVIL

However, when the evil one, Satan, is described, it is more than the mere absence of good, or rebellion against God's best. It's a spiritual presence of corruption and depravity completely opposed to God's nature and will. In Jesus' own words, the evil one's intent is stated like this: "The thief's purpose is to steal and kill and destroy" (John 10:10, *NLT*).

It perfectly describes the plan, as people become evildoers in unrepentant, premeditated acts like human trafficking that scheme to enslave, rape, kill or harm humanity for mere money or power. These acts bring us face to face not only with the evildoer, but with the Evil One.

And this kind of evil makes God angry.

Sometimes, because we believe so much in grace (I'm a grace, grace girl myself), we struggle with the image of an angry God. Yet, we are foolish if we ignore the reality that the evil one exists, or we believe that God is ambivalent about it.

The apostle Peter reminds us, "Stay alert! Watch out for your great enemy, the devil. He prowls around like a roaring lion, looking for someone to devour. Stand firm against him, and be strong in your faith" (1 Pet. 5:8-9, *NLT*).

Christ describes Satan as a "murderer from the beginning, not holding to the truth, for there is no truth in him. When he lies, he speaks his native language, for he is a liar and the father of lies" (John 8:44). He's a deceiver. A liar. An accuser. And that's the description of evil we often toss in with evil thoughts; broken behavior from broken people; temptation; or acting in a way that is contrary to God's hope and purpose for mankind, which is just confusing, especially for those harmed by evil.

A woman I met in Chicago named Marcia handed me a book and asked me to read her story. She's a teacher, a mom, a wife and a pastor's wife. As we sat I read, and what I read made me want to weep.[4]

As a child, Marcia was emotionally and physically beaten down nearly every day of her young life. Beginning at the age of four, she was placed in the hands of an older man her mother called "grandpa" (though he was no relation) to meet his sexual needs. Marcia was finally rescued and placed in the foster system. The authorities were amazed that so many people had overlooked the filth, the bruises and the scars on a tender little girl.

When she was an adult, she started sharing her story. For the most part, those she shared with grieved with her; but sometimes they just didn't know what to say. She received advice, like, "Forgive and forget." "Give it to God." "Be grateful for your husband (or your children) who love you deeply."

There was merit in these statements, but it placed the entire burden on her. If you are grateful enough, or you let go enough, somehow that will lead you to forgive and be healed.

For many, like Marcia, who have been harmed by evildoers, it is only when you realize that God is angry along with you over those evil acts that you can began to address the underlying emotions, scars and hurt. When you realize that God is angry for you, and along with you, you are no longer required to somehow absolve evil.

In their book *Shattered Soul?* authors Patrick Fleming and Sue Lauber-Fleming say that anger is a natural response to the aftermath of evil. But joining that anger with God's anger is the first step to healing.

> Your anger feels so strong, even destructive. You have witnessed or been victimized by the destructive power of anger. You have buried, repressed, or hidden your anger for years. Your anger has been directed mainly at yourself. Or you have let your anger flare out towards others in hurtful ways. All these ways at responding to the anger of abuse has kept you from tapping in to the potential healing of anger and blocked you from joining with God's anger. The purpose of God's anger is to restore and cleanse, not destroy or harm yourself or others.[5]

What Scripture Teaches About Evil

There are many places in Scripture that refer to evil, in both the Old and New Testaments. Jesus often spoke about evil. In Matthew 5, Jesus said:

> You have heard the law that says the punishment must match the injury: "An eye for an eye, and a tooth for a tooth." But I say, do not resist an evil person! If someone slaps you on the right cheek, offer the other cheek also (Matt. 5:38-39, *NLT*).

There is a powerful principle behind these verses, but understanding them in their context helps us know how to address evil.

Under the Law, punishment should match the crime. But the Pharisees, in what seemed to be a desire to live as holy a life as possible, had taken that specific rule and made it literal. If a person stole a loaf of bread, even if he was starving, the punishment was a severed hand; the punishment no longer matched the crime.

Once again, Jesus shakes up the disciples' thinking. Rather than an eye for an eye or a tooth for a tooth, He says that when you meet someone who is evil (and in this case, that word can mean a person who is stingy, a bad friend, one who exerts authority over you in the wrong manner, someone with wrong motives) and that person hits you on your right cheek or asks you for your coat or asks you to carry his baggage an extra mile, rather than meet violence with violence, you do the opposite.

You meet a stingy person with generosity.

You respond to a person who is overbearing with patience.

You meet malice with justice.

Not only was this contrary to the Pharisees' interpretation of the Law, but it also showed a peaceful response founded in love and introduced self-control and gentleness into an offense. Most of us would hit back or at least ball up our fists if someone struck us on the cheek. We would feel justified, and the rumble goes on.

But Jesus was saying don't meet bad behavior with bad behavior. Don't respond to evil with evil. When you turn the other cheek, your offender is presented with a choice. That surprising and peaceful response suddenly places the offender's actions in clear view, whether he want to see them or not. Perhaps he will strike your other cheek, but perhaps he'll be ashamed of his actions.

Regardless, Jesus was saying, you represent Me.

For a rough and tumble group of men, an eye for an eye probably felt like a much more comfortable response to an offense.

When Scripture addresses the evil one himself, there is a change in tone. In Revelation 20:10, we are granted a peek at a final reckoning:

> And the devil, who deceived them, was thrown into the lake of burning sulfur, where the beast and the false prophet had been thrown. They will be tormented day and night for ever and ever.

This is the response of a heavenly Father who loves but will recompense the Evil One for the destruction and havoc and harm he has poured out on the lives of God's beloved creation.

This is holy anger. Righteous anger.

It is anger that rises up in the heart of a Savior who speaks out when the Temple is desecrated (see Matt. 21:12); and how much more when the temple of His beloved creation is abused and harmed in such evil ways.

IF YOU'VE BEEN HURT BY EVIL

If you have encountered evil, though few may understand what you've faced, God feels sorrow that it took place. If there are people who have told you that what happened to you is God's will, or that somehow the end result was that God would somehow receive the glory, please understand that the evil one's purpose has never been for God to shine.

Your heavenly Father grieves over the pain you suffered, so much so that your Savior walked up the road willingly with stripes on His back, wore a crown of thorns pressed into His brow and suffered death on a cruel cross to offer healing and restoration. Sin and the plans of the evil one make Him righteously angry.

God is angry on your behalf.

Perhaps it seems impossible to hand that anger to something or someone else. Can we be honest about anger that resides so deeply that the evil one continues to destroy, kill and rob even when the offenders are no longer anywhere in sight? The rebuilding and healing process can be shattered by that anger which is too heavy for you to manage alone.

Let's return to Matthew 5:38, because it is just as powerful in your situation.

It is said that an eye for an eye or a tooth for a tooth . . .

Turning the other cheek means failing to meet evil with evil. This response is powerful resistance to the plan of the evil one. He thought he would steal from you, but you let God be angry for you and gained peace instead. He thought he would kill your spirit or your dreams, but you found renewed life and direction. He meant to destroy you, but God's redemptive power was unleashed as you let God handle the burden of anger for you.

Anger can be either a powerful tool to overcome evil or it can destroy what remains of your heart. Neither is it part of God's plan for His daughter. Let Him take that burden from you.

That doesn't mean you aren't allowed to be righteously angry. Righteous anger propels you to speak out against such evil. It leads you to join in with others who have bravely gone into the darkness to rescue children who are trapped in any number of evil endeavors. Going to the rescue gets done through prayer, funding and manpower.

Righteous anger can create a boldness to speak out against such evil, to move complacent or unaware believers to pray, support, encourage and stand with those who have been harmed by such evil.

Righteous anger also loosens the bonds of evil. When you bind your anger with God's, you are now free to embrace the truth that "nothing can ever separate you from God's love. Neither death nor life, neither angel nor demons, neither your fears for today nor

your worries about tomorrow—not even the powers of hell can separate you from God's love. No power in the sky above or in the
earth below—indeed, nothing in all creation will ever be able to
separate you from the love of God that is revealed in Christ Jesus
our Lord" (Rom. 8:38-39, *NLT*, pronouns adapted).

The plan of the evil one gets thwarted. He thought he had destroyed you, but instead your life is a reflection of John 10:10 in re-
verse: The enemy came to steal, kill and destroy . . . but My
purpose, God says, is to give you a rich and satisfying life.

Where does this new life lead you?

The answer to that question is as unique and diverse as you
are. For some, it leads to ministry with those in the same situation
you once were in. For others, it leads to solid Christian counsel to
mend the places that were wounded. For Corrie ten Boom, who
lost family members in the Holocaust and endured starvation, im-
prisonment and torture, it led her to 60-plus countries where she
shared the message that there is no pit so deep that God's love isn't
deeper still.

For some, healing and direction comes quickly, while others
offer up a layer at a time over years. Each way is valid and beautiful as God walks with you through the process.

In Marcia's case, her new life led her to share her story with
others, and to ignite women to first notice and then rescue children, just as an alert teacher once did for her. As a teacher herself,
Marcia found renewed purpose as she watches over all of those
who pass through her classroom.

Is There Forgiveness in the Case of Evil?

Forgiveness is always ours to offer. There are thousands of stories—from those of ordinary individuals to those whose stories
have shone in the spotlight. These people have forgiven under extraordinary circumstances, such as the massacres in Rwanda, the
Holocaust, slavery and other horrendous events. One of these people is Corrie ten Boom. In 1947, two years after the Allied Libera-

tion, ten Boom was speaking in Munich. A bald, heavy-set man in a gray overcoat, clutching a brown felt hat between his hands, walked toward Corrie. Suddenly the brown hat and gray overcoat faded away and she saw a blue uniform. She saw her sister Betsie's skeletal form. She saw the room with the dresses piled high.

When the man spoke, it was evident that he didn't recognize her, but he had heard her speak of Ravensbruck concentration camp. He told her that he was once a guard in that camp but had become a Christian, and he believed that God had forgiven him for the cruel things he did. He wondered if it was possible for her to forgive him.

He held out his hand. It hung between them as she wrestled with the most difficult thing she had ever been asked to do. Here's what she wrote about that moment:

> And still I stood there with the coldness clutching my heart. But forgiveness is not an emotion—I knew that too. Forgiveness is an act of the will, and the will can function regardless of the temperature of the heart. "Jesus, help me!" I prayed silently. "I can lift my hand, I can do that much. You supply the feeling."
>
> And so woodenly, mechanically, I thrust my hand into the one stretched out to me. And as I did, an incredible thing took place. The current started in my shoulder, raced down my arm, sprang into our joined hands. And then this healing warmth seemed to flood my whole being, bringing tears to my eyes. "I forgive you, brother!" I cried. "With all my heart!" For a long moment we grasped each other's hands, the former guard and the former prisoner. I had never known God's love so intensely as I did then.[6]

When Corrie reached out her hand, it was a gesture that demonstrated her trust in God, even as hatred rose in her heart. She prayed that God would meet her when their fingertips touched because she simply could not do it on her own. And He did.

Corrie ten Boom's forgiveness couldn't pardon the evil that took place in the Holocaust. Rather, it was an act of faith that embraced God's pardon for this one man's repentance; and in doing so, she was able to receive his apology and offer mercy.

Is forgiveness possible in the case of evil? "With man this is impossible, but with God all things are possible" (Matt. 19:26).

JUST YOU AND GOD

1. Why might we struggle to talk about evil and forgiveness?

2. Read 1 Peter 5:8. How is Satan described? How might holding on to anger leave a person defenseless?

3. Describe someone you know who has been marked by evil, but who met evil with a surprising response. What does that person's example teach you?

4. What might it look like to allow God's righteous anger to take the place of your own?

_____

_____

_____

_____

5. Read Romans 12:9-21. Perhaps you've never encountered evil as discussed in this chapter. How are we to respond to evil in our community or our world?

_____

_____

_____

_____

_____

6. What does it mean to "weep with those who weep" (v. 15, *NLT*)?

_____

_____

_____

_____

7. What does it mean to "never pay back evil with more evil" (v. 17, *NLT*)?

_____

_____

_____

_____

PRINCIPLE

God is angry for you.

To Forgive

Allow God's holy anger to take your burden.

Prayer

Father, today I am convinced that nothing can separate me from Your love. Not evil. Not wickedness. I've been angry, and You understand my anger. You don't condemn my feelings, but you do offer freedom from living bound by them. I don't know where healing might take me, but I do know it will be hand-in-hand with You.

Notes

1. Christine Caine, *Undaunted: Doing What God Calls You to Do* (Grand Rapids, MI: Zondervan, 2012), pp. 11-14.
2. Stewart Burns, "Humankind's Most Savage Cruelty," *Sojourners*, February 2012.
3. Kay Arthur, *When Hurt Runs Deep: Healing and Hope for Life's Desperate Moments* (Colorado Springs, CO: Waterbrook Press, 2010).
4. Margaret Sweeney, comp. *Pearl Girls: Encountering Grit, Experiencing Grace* (Chicago: Moody Publishers, 2009), p. 41.
5. Patrick Fleming, Sue Lauber-Fleming and Vicki S. Schmidt, *Shattered Soul? Five Pathways to Healing the Spirit After Abuse and Trauma* (Nashville, TN: Wordstream Publishing, 2011), p. 80.
6. Corrie ten Boom, *The Hiding Place* (Grand Rapids, MI: Chosen Books, 2006).

11

You Live in Grace

I turn my hands over, spread my fingers open. I receive grace. And through me, grace could flow on. Like a cycle of water, in continuous movement grace is meant to fall, a rain . . . again, again, again.

Ann Voskamp, *1000 Gifts*

A few years ago on my birthday, my husband and I climbed in the car. He asked me to shut my eyes and keep them closed. We drove a short while and stopped.

"Open your eyes," he said.

We were parked in front of a small tattoo parlor.

"You've always wanted this." He pulled out a sheet of paper. "I found this on the Internet. It's *grace* in Hebrew. Let's do this. I want to give you this tattoo for your birthday."

It's true. I had always wanted a small wrist tattoo, but . . .

I stand in front of people and teach the Bible. Sometimes that image is on a large screen, and I use my hands when I speak. Though I had wanted this tattoo for several years, my fear is that someone somewhere would be offended by the tattoo, and that offense would cause them to get tripped up. It's not in my nature to worry about what others think, but I wanted to be sensitive.

"You could explain why you have it," he said.

Fifteen minutes later the small tattoo marched across my wrist.

The first time I spoke, I wore a bracelet that covered it. While I was speaking, it slipped and as I shared the message the tiny tattoo flashed several times. Afterwards, several young women came up. "We have to know what it means," they said.

"It is Hebrew script for grace," I said. "Every time I hold my hands up in worship, it's a reminder of what God has done for me. He's marked my life with grace. I can't help but be grateful for that amazing gift."

From that day forward, I no longer tried to hide it. If I wore a bracelet, it's because it was pretty and I liked it; but there was no disguising this very small, very personal token of love between my God and me.

Since that time I've discovered that I should have hesitated before receiving the tattoo. My husband diligently copied Hebrew script from the Internet. Surprised by his thoughtfulness, it never occurred to me that his research might not result in the right word. Technically, it sounds out grace but looks more like the word "quilt," nothing like either the Hebrew or Greek words for grace.

But it's still beautiful to me.

When I lift my hands to praise Him, it's still a reminder of His mercy and immense love, His grace that has been present from the time I was in chaos as a little girl to an angry teen to the woman I have become.

FORGIVING OURSELVES WHEN WE FALL SHORT

Go as deep into Scripture as you want and you will not find where you or I have the ability to forgive ourselves. That's a concept that isn't scriptural, and yet it's discussed often.

You've got to forgive yourself.

You've got to make a fresh start.

We have something so much greater. We have grace. When we ask God for pardon, for mercy, we find it.

But there's more!

The apostle John reminds us that we aren't alone in our daily lives. The Holy Spirit knows the will and plan of God for each of us; but He also knows our intentions, our thoughts and our desires to love and serve God. When we fall short, and we repent,

He is our advocate. When we are temped or start to go the wrong way, the Holy Spirit is there to remind us of who we belong to and brings to mind everything Christ has spoken through Scripture and through relationship (see John 14:26).

To be honest, there are times when I have ignored that gentle nudge inside (or the hammering in my heart). I've plunged head-on into arguments because I'm angry or it serves my purpose or I've just lost self-control and it feels good in the moment.

Those are the moments when repentance and grace lead me back to who and where I'm supposed to be.

> **χάρις** [Greek] translated *charis:* (1) graciousness; (2) the divine influence upon the heart, and its reflection in the life, including *gratitude*; (3) acceptable; (4) favor or gift; (5) joy or liberality.

GRACE, GRACE, WONDERFUL GRACE

In John 1:19-27, when Jewish leaders met with John the Baptist in Bethany, located across the Jordan River, they asked him pointedly, "Who are you? Are you Elijah?"

John replied, "I am not."

The leaders then asked, "Are you the Prophet?"

Again, John answered no.

So the leaders said to him, "Why then do you baptize if you are not the Messiah, nor Elijah, nor the Prophet?"

John replied, "I baptize with water . . . but among you stands one you do not know. He is the one who comes after me, the straps of whose sandals I am not worthy to untie" (vv. 26-27).

Earlier in John 1, the Gospel writer tells us who John the Baptist was speaking about: "All who did receive him, to those who believed in his name, he gave the right to become children of God—children born not of natural descent, nor of human decision or a husband's will, but born of God" (John 1:12-13).

John the Baptist was preaching a fine sermon, but it's clear the leaders didn't understand his message. And why should they? These men had been toiling away for years to be good enough, right enough, learned enough to earn their way out of sin and into God's favor. They had heaped on traditions and restrictions, and the thought of a simple act of belief being sufficient just seemed silly, or worse, blasphemous.

Just moments before Jesus stepped into public ministry, John told these men, "Out of his fullness we have *all* received grace in place of grace already given. For the law was given through Moses; grace and truth came through Jesus Christ" (John 1:16, emphasis added).

In *THE MESSAGE,* it is stated like this: "We all live off his generous bounty, gift after gift after gift."

One commentator notes that "grace in place of grace" is an unusual expression, as it describes the idea of continuance and an inexhaustible supply of God's grace to believers. No wonder John's statement confounded the religious leaders. How could they fathom a source that is never interrupted and knows no bounds?

I fear that many times we are just like the Pharisees.

We can be the good ones trying to be perfect, wearing a mask that hides the fact that we often feel less than perfect. We can run from God, thinking there is no way we can be accepted. We might shout out to God and then fear that we are too honest with our words. We do wrong things, and then we believe we can hide from God, just far enough away that we want grace but think we will never receive it.

When I receive a gift, I rip the paper off as soon as it's placed in my hands. I treasure gifts because they were handpicked just for me, even if it's a tattoo that looks like "quilt" instead of "grace."

And yet, we often hold grace at a distance.

Grace is the unmerited favor and pleasure of God for each of us, which not only draws us close to our heavenly Father but also results in a divine influence upon the heart and reflection in each life that produces a life of gratitude.

So why is grace so hard to accept?

Why We Might Struggle to Accept Grace

Sometimes we might struggle to accept grace because of a pain-filled past and what we learned during that time.

Counselor and therapist Robert Burney, M.A., defined four roles a child can take on when raised in dysfunction. He calls these roles the Hero, the Scapegoat, the Lost Child and the Mascot. There's a fifth role that sometimes crops up when speaking of these, and that is the Caretaker or Peacemaker.

It was Burney's belief that we take on as defense mechanisms the roles that best suit our personality.[1] I first heard this teaching nearly two decades ago at a conference. As I listened, I could clearly identify where I, and my siblings, landed as we grew up.

The first role is the Rebel or Scapegoat. The rebel speaks out, even if it leads to unfair or abusive punishment. He or she beats everyone to the punch as far as behavior is concerned. *You say I'm bad? Let me show you bad.*

No one gets to do anything to you that you aren't already doing to yourself. Like Stephanie (in chapter 7), the rebel might look for love in the wrong places or numb pain in whatever manner works the quickest; and he or she has the most fun doing it. All the while the rebel is still yelling out what's wrong, no matter how much trouble it brings him or her.

This can cause the rebel to become the Scapegoat. The rest of the family says, *If she'd straighten up, we'd be all right.* In some cases, the rebel is the only one brave enough to tell the truth in the dysfunctional family.

Another response is to be the Hero, or the good girl. The good girl/hero tosses out mom's cigarettes; hides dad's booze; makes good grades. She does and says everything right. If someone around the hero isn't toeing the line, it's not unusual for the hero to tell on him or her. The hero believes the less trouble she is in, the more chance she has to make it in the chaotic environment in which she lives.

When others look at the hero, it makes her family feel better. *We couldn't have been all that bad to turn out someone so good.*

Then there is the Lost Child. She almost disappears. This child can be seen as "good" because she doesn't get in the way. She's learned that if she escapes notice, she just might escape trouble. She is there, but she might as well be invisible.

The next is the Mascot, or Clown. She's entertaining. She's the funny one. Her witticism might be inappropriate, but she's funny. It's how she deflects painful situations. Humor becomes her M.O.

Then there is the Caretaker or Peacemaker. Some put the Mascot and Caretaker together, but others say they are separate roles. The peacemaker or caretaker is where I believe I landed. The caretaker is not necessarily the good girl, because she'll step into the line of fire. She speaks her mind, but with peace as the objective. She may or may not take care of her parent(s), but she's there for her siblings. She may even attempt to take responsibility of the emotional wellbeing of her family.

The problem with each of these roles is that no child has the maturity or the ability to fix a broken family dynamic. Second, and most important, you can get stuck in these roles. They may linger 10, 15, 20-plus years. The Rebel is still rebelling. The Hero is still the good girl, perhaps even the perfect one everyone admires. The Mascot is still the funny one. The Lost child is still hiding. The Caretaker is still trying to fix everyone or make everyone play fair or get along.

Do you remember earlier that I shared the things I find hard to forgive?

Each one of them is linked to that role I took on as a child. I want everyone to get along. I want to make sure no one gets hurt. But years ago, I put down that role.

It's not mine to hold.

My only roles are mom, wife, sister, daughter, grandma and friend. Other than those, I'm just supposed to be uniquely Suzie. There will always be the aspect of the peacemaker or caregiver inside of me; it's a groove that runs deep. And in appropriate doses, it's healthy. But it's not who I am.

That's where grace comes in.

As you heal, whether it is in a counselor's office or through the great Counselor Himself, you might struggle to forgive yourself because of the influence of those roles you took on as a child and never put down. I have sat with thousands of women and heard these words:

I stuff it all down. I have never given myself permission to talk about what happened.

You see, the good girl doesn't make waves.

I did so many bad things. Yes, my past is ugly, but the ugliest parts I brought on myself.

The rebel ran so hard into the arms of whatever it took to numb her pain that now she doesn't feel worthy of God's grace. She's been honest with God, and because of that honesty she fears that He might see her like everyone else, as the troublemaker.

My standards are so high that it's impossible for me to ever feel anything but guilt.

The caretaker or peacemaker has placed her standards so high that even she can't reach them.

I don't think God even sees me.

If she's funny enough, entertaining enough, witty enough, maybe God will notice her. But so far it doesn't seem to be working. Let's tap dance a little harder, shall we?

How can God love someone so mad at Him?

She wants to come out of isolation, but to do so means she's going to have to be honest, even noticed. She'll have to express her feelings. That's scary stuff.

Charis grace refers to something delightful or beautiful in a person or thing. The Holy Spirit sees beneath the guise of the rebel, or the good girl, or the girl trying to make everyone happy to the person beneath. And God isn't afraid or dismayed by our honesty, or unaware of our attempts to find our way closer to Him.

He's been reaching for you your entire life.

Charis means to offer a favor or a gift that brings pleasure to another. The reason I wanted grace etched on my wrist in small script is because of the vast impact it had on this once caregiving, peacemaking little girl I was. You see, I had no way of making things better. I could take my little brothers with me when I went out with friends so they could be in a safe place. I could tell them stories at night when life was chaotic. I could stand in front of a swinging belt and take the sting intended for my baby brother.

But years later, when marked by grace instead of a belt, I still struggled daily to think that I was doing enough to make God happy. What a trick of the enemy! It not only created an impossible bar, but it also conflicted with knowing God and thus the discovery process He had for me.

Do you realize that you bring pleasure to God? Yes, *you.* Right where you are. He sees your heart. He sees your potential.

Charis also means to be grateful.

How can we not express thankfulness and praise when we realize that we can put down roles and masks and striving to embrace Him.

GRACE IN REAL LIFE

Because I struggled, years ago I decided to study grace and discover how I could live in it. Those findings reshaped my relationship with God when grace became more than a theory.

Each day when I woke up, I spent time with my heavenly Father, not out of duty but because time with Him and in His presence changes me. When I walked into that place, it was without guilt, without hang-ups. That was a conscious choice on my part.

Today, when I walk into this secret place (see Matt. 6:6), I do so knowing that God knows what I need before I even ask (see v. 8). If yesterday was hard, He already knows that; so I offer up every part of that day to Him. If I struggled, He already knows that; so I hold up those struggles and ask for insight and wisdom. If I am joyous, I don't hold back that joy but celebrate it with Him.

Each day is a new opportunity to love Him and walk with Him. When I fail, and I do, it isn't an opportunity to heap guilt or obsess over that failure, because there's no merit in that. It's an opportunity to walk into the Source of grace and ask for forgiveness as I honestly repent of my sin and ask for direction and grace to do better.

And this is the place where *charis* transforms me the most from the little girl trying to make everyone and everything work out. I understand that my response as a child of God is to do what He asks me to do. It clears up the clutter. I have Scripture to guide me. The Holy Spirit lives inside of me.

It's absolutely freeing!

Many times it actually takes me further outside my comfort zone as I trust His leading and hear and recognize His voice, and follow where He leads (see John 10:27). It might lead to a hurting woman who doesn't know that Jesus loves her. It might lead to writing a book about forgiveness, even as you fear that people will ask you questions you are not equipped to answer. It might lead to holding my tongue because I feel that gentle nudge that says, "Don't react in anger, sis." But in each of these everyday and bigger moments, I know the only true Source is Jesus, and I point to Him.

I wish I could tell you step-by-step how grace works, but in this case, I'm not much different from the man who said, "But I know this: I was blind, and now I can see!" (John 9:25, *NLT*). Living in grace changes who you are.

You stop trying to forgive yourself—an impossible task—and you shift the focus to total receptivity of His grace. It's a gift that you not only receive, but you give. As you receive it, you are able to pour it out on others.

GRACE OFFERS PURPOSE

Grace (*charis*) gives you permission to find your place.

For me, that's as a teacher—whether sitting with a small group of women in a Bible study, writing, blogging, or speaking in a larger setting. It's a natural passion and love. I am free to find my place in my family and in my interactions with others.

Grace in place of grace.

I drop the legalistic law that says I have to be perfect, and I follow Christ instead, which influences my relationships and allows me to function fully in the ways that God made me. It drops every pretense. My relationship with God is born out of relationship and adoration and gratitude and obedience to Him.

GRACE OFFERS POWER

His Grace offers power not only to forgive ourselves when we fall short, but it also takes away our sin, removing it as far as the east is from the west. It breaks down all the barriers between you and your heavenly Father.

I need grace as I parent. I need grace as I love my husband. I need grace as I stand in front of a crowd or try to make a writing deadline or juggle all the things that I love best. Grace gives me clarity when things don't work out as I think they should, because I know that I've done all that I can.

And when I fail, the power that flows from the exalted Christ cleanses my sin and puts me back on the path I am meant to run with joy. It's this power that Luke describes in Acts 4:33: "And God's grace was so powerfully at work in them all," revealing a crowd of ordinary people doing extraordinary things in His name.

GRACE SAVES US

I remember the girl in eighth grade who was so angry that she almost exploded out the library doors. The heavy metal doors slammed into the concrete blocks with a bang. The teacher rushed down the hall in pursuit and pushed the girl against the wall with her elbow against her chest. The girl didn't care if the teacher was angry. She didn't care that she had to go to the office or that she would pick up trash around school for the next several days after school.

That same girl, at 13, nestled into dark corners at the skating rink in the arms of a boy who would ignore her the next day at school; but she was willing to make out with him anyway because it made her feel wanted.

She was the young girl, at 16, who knelt at an altar and wept, and then ran home to tell her parents the news that she was "saved," though her family had no idea what that meant.

She became the young mom who wanted nothing more than to give her children safety and stability and laughter, and who often felt overwhelmed with three babies under the age of two.

She is the same woman who drove down the highway recently, her heart heavy because she thought she had done everything right only to discover there was work to be done in a relationship.

In each of these instances, God's grace saved me. I don't know where I would be without His grace. I look at the young girl in the arms of the boy, or the angry teen who wanted to fight anyone and everyone, and I see a God who poured out grace over her life as she wept in a small church in Tulsa, Oklahoma. He rescued me, and that grace continues today. It's a rescue of the sort that pulls you up out of a pit, whether of your own making or not.

As a girl, I had no idea of the gift God wanted to give me. As a young mom, I had started to grasp it.

But the woman driving that car? She knows exactly where to go. She invites the Holy Spirit into the moment, knowing that God's grace is sufficient, and there's help to be found in that truth alone.

As we live day to day, there are going to be those opportunities and hard places; but His grace marches into them with you. Your heavenly Father finds pleasure in you as you trust Him, living life in tandem with Him with the assistance of the Holy Spirit, bathed in grace.

GRACE IS NOT PERMISSION TO SIN

This poured-out gift is not given so that we might handle it carelessly. It's not permission to walk boldly into sin or to take advantage. The apostle Paul encourages us: "What shall we say, then? Shall we go on sinning so that grace may increase? By no means! We are those who have died to sin; how can we live in it any longer?" (Rom. 6:1-2).

When you receive grace as the priceless gift that it is, you receive a repentant, contrite heart in return. You are grateful for what you have, and breaking God's heart on purpose is not where you want to go.

GRACE HEALS

A woman named Cynthia had married, given birth to children, and was active in church. She loved others in a special way.[2] She was known as a giving person, and a great mom.

Cynthia had a secret. Her father had repeatedly molested her when she was a child.

Though she gave grace to others, privately she rarely offered it to herself. As she baked cookies for her children's classroom, opened her home for Bible study and created a comfortable co-coon for her family, she carried her burden alone. Her secret drove her to dark despair. One day, she finally broke down and shared that secret with her husband.

He was a good man and tried his best to love her through the dark places. They sought counsel. Their pastor offered steps to help her deal with her depression.

But it wasn't working.

In the morning, after her kids left for school, she closed the shades and burrowed deeper into her pain. She wept over her mixed feelings for her husband as he reached out to her, struggling to admit that she didn't feel worthy of that measure of love, but also resenting that he was trying to fix her. In her journal, she wrote these words:

I'm worthless.

No one could possibly love me if they really knew me.

She continued to bake cookies, meals and make her children feel loved. She tried to be the perfect partner in ministry and in the home.

When people looked at their family, it was with respect.

However, the harder she worked to be the opposite of the message playing out in her thoughts, the greater the shame. One day, she found a quiet place on the deck in her backyard and began talking to God.

God, I can't do this anymore. I've forgiven, but I still hurt.

As she closed her eyes, God showed her a little girl. The little girl was huddled on the back porch, afraid. Suddenly, she felt a whisper inside.

"Come play, child."

As she sat with her eyes closed, she felt that God was holding out His hands. When she took them, He led her to a playground and they jumped rope together. They swung high in the air on a swing set. When playtime was over, He led her to the porch. She looked down at the dress she was wearing.

It was brand new.

When she opened her eyes, she recognized her shattered little girl self and began to weep for her. She had done nothing wrong, but the message that she was soiled was so indelibly imprinted on her heart that she had walked through life seeing herself as unworthy. The harder she worked and tried to be the best in everything, the more she pushed down her secret and the more it hurt.

As she sat on the deck that day, she understood for the first time that no one—not her husband nor any other person—could be God. No one could fill that place inside of her. Counseling with her pastor was helpful. Journaling helped. Her husband's love had given her a glimpse of God's love; but only God could fill the shattered places left by an earthly father.

It's been several years since that personal prayer encounter.

Cynthia is no longer bound by a secret; she is bathed in grace. Just like before, she reaches out to women. Just like before, many people love her. But the difference now is that she realizes she is worth that love.

I heard Cynthia's story in a church one night many years ago. She's not a speaker, but she stood on the stage and shared openly. She wept, not out of sadness but out of joy. I also watched women respond to her message, a few finding their way to the front of the church as they knelt and unburdened their own secrets and held up their hands in worship as they received the grace that had been waiting all along.

Perhaps it's inconceivable to you, as it was to me that night, that a little girl who was so innocent, so good and so hurt by another person's sin, might be in such great need of grace. But in this instance, grace [*charis*] was all of the definitions mixed into one.

It was a divine influence upon the heart.

It was a reflection of her life as seen through God's point of view.
It was a gift.

The receiver accepted it.

Like Cynthia, you might strive to make others see you on the
exterior or to prove that you are worthy. Maybe you are seen as the
perfect wife, perfect mother, perfect [fill-in-the-blank], but you feel
like it's a facade. Hebrews 4:16 invites all of us to "approach God's
throne of grace with confidence, so that we may receive mercy and
find grace [*charis*] to help us in our time of need."

His grace is sufficient. Today that gift is available for you, and
it's there tomorrow as well. As you receive that gift, you start discovering, exploring and settling comfortably into your skin, knowing to whom you belong: You are a daughter of the King—covered
by and wrapped in His grace.

JUST YOU AND GOD

1. How hard have you been trying to forgive yourself? How does
   grace change that endeavor?

   _____

   _____

   _____

   _____

   _____

2. In 2 Corinthians 12:8-9, Paul is reminded, and he reminds us,
   that even in a weak or vulnerable place, God's grace is sufficient
   (plenty, enough). In which areas do you desire grace the most?

   _____

   _____

   _____

   _____

3. Is there a role that you played as a child as a defense mechanism? How does that role continue to play out today? How can grace help you put that role down?

_____

_____

_____

_____

_____

4. Read Romans 8:27. How can the Holy Spirit draw you closer to God?

_____

_____

_____

_____

_____

5. If you unwrap the gift of grace today, what might that look like in real life tomorrow? How would it change the way you relate to God? How would it change the way you view yourself?

_____

_____

_____

_____

_____

CHARIS PRINCIPLE

You are offered a free gift with a divine influence upon the heart.

TO *CHARIS* FORGIVE

Open that gift daily.

Suzanne Eller

PRAYER

Savior, Today I stand before You cleansed and made whole by Your gift of grace. I do not take it lightly, but rather I hold it close as a generous and outpoured gift. Let me live in it. Let me offer it to others, but also to myself. Thank You for the Holy Spirit, who knows me and knows Your heart for my life.

Notes

1. Robert Burney, M.A., "Roles in Dysfunctional Families," Addictions.net. www.addictions.net/id279.html.
2. Not her real name.

PART 3

What's Next?

1 2

Live as a Forgiver

God, interrupt whatever we are doing so that we can join ou in what You're doing.

Francis Chan

Now that you have considered all of the bigger issues you might face when you forgive, are you ready to live a forgiving lifestyle? If so, can I make you a promise?

It's not easy.

I know, I should have told you something like, "From this moment forward you are going to be known as the most forgiving human being on earth. You'll wake up each day with a heart filled with grace for yourself and others."

Except it doesn't work like that. You will still have ample opportunities to forgive, even after you've climbed over that monumental forgiveness mountain that once stood in the way. You'll still have that condescending boss. You'll still be in proximity with that person who says all the wrong things, or at least it feels that way. You'll still have those days when you are the one struggling with self-control.

Not only that, but in your lifetime, you will face something that seems impossible to forgive . . . again.

Though I can't promise that a forgiving lifestyle is easy, I can share with you that it's freeing.

A couple of years ago, I went zip-lining. I have a fear of heights. I think it has something to do with the fact that my dad held my little brother over the Grand Canyon when he was 3, and I was 10, and I completely panicked, thinking my brother would tumble over the side and be gone forever.

Regardless of how it arrived, the fear was real.

My son bought a zip-lining package for two on Groupon so that I could put a checkmark on my bucket list next to "get over my fear of heights." When we arrived at the outdoor zip-lining facility, I noticed several towers, zigzagging zip-lines and people harnessed in a series of hitches and buckles. My heart immediately started thumping overtime. After our harnesses were in place and we'd made a couple of low-line practice runs, we were asked to climb a reasonably high tower.

Now this was the hard part.

The stairway was circular, metal, and open from the waist up. The higher I climbed the more my brain informed me that I was afraid. I felt light-headed, but I was determined and just kept putting one foot in front of the other. Up, up, up.

We stood at the top of the first tower. My son zip-lined first and soared from one tower to the next with ease. Then I stepped up. I had already mentioned to the guides that I was afraid of heights. "Not just afraid, but really, really terrified," I said, just in case they didn't get it. I stepped onto the small platform and almost froze. The platform was tiny. One inch in front of me there was nothing between me and the ground . . . hundreds of feet below.

I put my gloved hands on the zip-line. To be frank, I wasn't sure I could do it. Everything in me was screaming this was foolish, that it was frightening, and to turn around and go back to solid ground.

But then I let go . . . and it was exhilarating!

I flew through the air. I laughed. I slid in smoothly to the next tower where my son fist-pumped in the air with a "Way to go, Mom!"

And then there was another tower, and a bridge. Each was a little higher, a little shakier, and it required a lot more faith and confidence. There was a moment when I stood in the middle of a rope-and-plank bridge as the wind whipped me around that I nearly fainted with fear; but then there were those "letting go" moments, and they were totally worth the harder parts.

A few weeks later, I was in a high-rise building and stepped out on the balcony. I held on to the rail and looked down at the stun-

ning view below. And then it hit me. I wasn't afraid. Before I zip-
lined, I couldn't have stood near the edge of the balcony, and I definitely wouldn't have peered over to see the scene beneath.

So much had been gained in the hard parts of conquering
my fear.

Yes, it's true that living as a forgiver isn't easy. It goes against
how we feel. It goes against cultural beliefs. Sometimes it just
doesn't make sense, not in the natural.

But there is so much to be gained in the harder parts of forgiving. You learn to release or overcome things that once kept you
stuck or afraid or angry, and you soar.

Instead of weak, you become strong. You also learn to choose
your battles. You weigh what is valid, and some issues simply aren't
worth the investment of time, energy, thought process and emo-
tion; so you don't engage in "word-fare" with others or try to hammer your point until he or she "gets it through his (or her) thick
head." You see, it's not that you've become passive, but you are no
longer passive-aggressive. You are intentional.

By doing this, you discover how to address the real problems
with people and events. You also grasp the art of responding rather
than reacting as you perfect the art of the pause, giving your emotions a chance to simmer down before you say or do something,
because you have discovered that words and behavior matter.
You've always known that, but now your life reflects it.

You also find grace for yourself, and for others.

As you begin this new or deeper journey as a forgiver, it's important to understand some really important principles.

You Understand That Forgiving Doesn't Make You a Saint

Forgiving doesn't change who you are. If you are witty, salty,
gentle-hearted, sarcastic (in a good way) or matter of fact, you
are still you.

Forgiving is a deep-inside transformation that helps you look
at life and people in a different way. You don't become Saint Suzie,

and you aren't perfect. In fact, living as a forgiver is only a reminder of how much grace is poured out on each of us by Christ, and somehow that translates into compassion and, eventually, patience.

But you are still you—just a kinder, gentler and more self-controlled you.

Forgiving is not an art. It's an attitude of the heart that evolves over time and with practice. It becomes a part of you.

It cannot be one more thing on your to-do list or a hoop you have to jump through. It's a choice to allow Christ to love through you and in you, and to forgive you and equip you as you follow Him imperfectly, as the Holy Spirit teaches you over and again in each situation or with each new opportunity.

Paul tells us, in Ephesians, that there is so much more for us as believers: "I pray that the eyes of your heart may be enlightened in order that you may know the . . . incomparably great power for us who believe" (Eph. 1:18-19). When we live as a forgiver, we discover what this verse means. God's power is woven into our relationships, our interactions, our faith, our purpose and the direction we take as we live life in an entirely different way than yesterday.

You Believe the Best Before Assuming the Worst

In an earlier chapter, I shared how believing the best helped me to begin a fresh start with a loved one. It's just as powerful a tool as you continue to practice and live out forgiveness. Sometimes a misunderstanding may arise out of a need for better communication. It may come from an oversight or someone who is completely unaware of her offense. Yet all too often we charge in believing the worst.

She's insensitive.

She meant to hurt me.

She must be out to get me.

The outcome of this mentality sets up any hope for conflict resolution at a big fat zero. Has that ever happened to you? Someone comes at you and suddenly you are on the defensive. You aren't sure what you've done wrong (or maybe you know exactly what you've done), but because this person jumped to the worst conclusion, you are on the defensive. It's a terrible place to start from when you are trying to work things out.

What if you believe the best, but that person proves otherwise? Well, then you have the real problem to deal with rather than the imaginary one you might have created in your thoughts by believing the worst.

You Need to Choose Your Battles

One night, I received a phone call from an acquaintance. "I need to tell you something," she said. "Someone is saying bad things about you, and I thought you should know."

"Is it something that could harm my marriage or my children?" I asked.

"No, it's about you. It's really bad."

"Did I do something unintentional to hurt someone's feelings?"

"No, it's about you! She's the one doing and saying wrong things, telling everyone that . . ."

"Then I don't want to know, but thank you for caring. I love that you want to protect me."

I sensed her confusion. "But don't you want to know who it is?" she asked.

"No, I don't," I said. "I know who I am to my husband and to my children. But most of all, I know who I am when I am alone with God, and all of those things are in a good place. She may just be having a bad day, or maybe she's hurting. But again, I appreciate you loving me enough to want to protect me. That's awesome."

When the phone call ended, I went on with my day. I truly did not want to know what was said or who said it. If I hurt someone, yes, I would want to know that; but to chase rumors or confront someone over what she said so that I could feel justified or in the right, there was no reason to do that.

I know who I am.

To this day, years later, I don't know who that person is or how that situation resolved, but I do know that I'm glad for the guidance the Holy Spirit gently offered during that phone call.

We have choices to make. Battles to pick. What would happen if hurtful or unintentional comments were left to simmer and then fizzle out because no one poured accelerant on the embers? Some battles are absolutely necessary to work through, while others are time stealers, robbing us of time and energy we can devote to things that are of more value.

You Have to Resolve or Deal with Conflict

Conflict isn't going to go away. Even if you've resolved your own feelings, there's still an uncomfortable situation or person that will be a very real part of your life.

A new friend and I were chatting when she alluded to her father, one of many references she made throughout our time together. Right before we were to part, she told me a story. She had gone to eat Sunday dinner with her parents, and her father berated her during the entire meal.

"Is that normal?" I asked.

She nodded. "It happens every single time. This has gone on for years."

"What is he angry about?" I asked.

"He says that I don't love God. He uses the Bible to tell me how wrong I am."

Though I had known my friend for only a short time, she appeared to be a great mom and wife, and it was apparent that she loved Christ very much.

"Do you think your father is right in what he is saying?" I asked.

"It's not the truth at all."

"Have you told him that?"

She shook her head. "I never say anything. I just sit there until he's through."

"What is the effect on you and your family?"

She sighed. "My children hate going to see their grandparents. My husband has refused to go at all, even at holidays. He continually asks me why I allow my father to treat me in that way, and why I go back."

"How do you answer him?"

She looked up in surprise. "I say that I want to honor my dad. I want to respect him."

"*Do* you respect him?"

She was quiet for a moment, then she looked up with tears in her eyes. "There are times when I am so hurt and angry at my dad because of how he is affecting my marriage. It messes with the way I see myself and, sadly, it affects the way I view God sometimes. I honestly feel that if my own dad thinks this way, then I must be doing something wrong."

My friend felt that forgiveness meant to avoid conflict and accept verbal battering in front of her children. Though she grieved over the impact on her children and marriage, she felt biblically bound to respect her father by continuing to show up without any hope of resolving conflict.

It was an "aha" moment when she realized that what was taking place was far from respectful or God honoring on any level. Her father was hurtful and lacked insight on the damage that he was causing.

The words she felt in her heart and said in her head all the way home every Sunday were far from respectful or honoring.

Over time, my friend took positive steps. First, she tried to see things his way, not to make them right or wrong, but to gain perspective. Due to his strict religious background, he saw his daughter as in continual danger of losing her way. He did love her, but his love was shown in an unhealthful manner. He wasn't a totally bad person. He couldn't be defined only by their dinner conversations.

But she also acknowledged that remaining silent was damaging in many ways, especially to her children and her marriage.

She had several options: She could speak the truth; she could engage in an extended argument over religious differences; she could get angry and lash out; she could end the relationship; she could continue on without change.

Before talking with her father, she redefined her definition of honoring her father to having a truthful relationship rather than one that was one-sided and created unresolved anger and bitterness.

The next time her father berated her, she asked him to go to another room with her. There she said, "Dad, I'm sorry that you believe I have made wrong choices, but it's not the way I see it. I'm a good person, and I love God very much. I love you, but it's not right for me or for my children or for my marriage that I allow you to say those things. I'd like our relationship to be one of mutual respect and love. I want to be here, but I'm afraid I'll have to leave any time that happens."

In a perfect world, her father would have apologized and family dinners would have been peaceful. But we don't live in a perfect world. Her father saw it as impertinence and, in anger, he told her how disappointed he was in her words and in her.

She left. Not in anger. Not with a need to prove him wrong.

The conflict was no longer brushed under the rug, but in full view. She had gently given her dad fair warning that his actions were no longer acceptable without losing her temper, and she affirmed her love for her father in the process.

Have things changed? Yes and no. Her father still believes he is right, and his daughter has tried to understand how he gained those beliefs. After a few times of quietly leaving when her father started in with inappropriate and hurtful words, he eventually stopped.

It's not tranquil, but it's a small step in the right direction.

It is progress; and that's something else to remember as you live as a forgiver. It's not always going to be smooth or easy or tied up in a nice, neat bow. Loving people is a messy process. But if there is progress, even if it's a baby step, it's worth celebrating.

In my new friend's case, working through conflict has been transforming. It improved her marriage. Her husband says that he is learning from her how to be respectful and how to honor relationships, because he just wanted to storm out or let her dad have it. Her children feel protected instead of forced to listen to confusing messages about God and a person's worth. And she no longer pushes conflict down, down, down. When she looks in the mirror, she sees what was there all along—a strong woman of faith who tries to do the right thing and who loves her family. Her father's words have begun to lose their potency.

You Practice Gratitude Therapy

When I found out that I had cancer as a young mom, my life completely altered. Everything slowed down as I tried to heal, undergo chemotherapy and radiation and two surgeries. Nearly a year after treatment, things I had been too busy to notice suddenly were in clear view. My children were young and noisy and loving, but they also fought with each other in the van, my son poking his twin sister if she got too close. Before my diagnosis, I treasured my children, but there were a thousand little things I wasn't that grateful for, like the sibling rivalry or the mountain of laundry I tackled after work every night.

But afterwards, I listened to their laughter and their silly jokes, and I was thankful. I folded the laundry, their small hands joining in to help, and I was grateful.

After cancer, I noticed how great key lime pie tasted. I was grateful for the lush flowers blooming in the park. I was thankful for my husband's arms around my neck, and for my mother's voice when she called to say hello.

Don't get me wrong.

I still had bills to pay. I still dealt with difficult people, and I even had loved ones who made my heart hurt at times. There were numerous opportunities for offense, to jump back into the pit I had climbed out of or to look at the negative of my life, like chemotherapy, hospital bills, a changed body or going through menopause at the ripe "old" age of 32, due to treatment and surgery.

But gratitude helped me to see the miracles instead of the mountain.

Ann Voskamp, in her book *1000 Gifts,* shares that she was hungry to live life well. She wanted to find joy in the midst of deadlines, drama, six children and her past experiences, such as the tragic loss of a sister.

She wanted God in her day, whether it was dark, gritty and long, or joy-filled. She began a spiritual discipline of numbering God's gifts to her, expressing gratitude for each one every day. By doing so, she says that she discovered the life she always wanted in the life she already had.

She discovered it simply by expressing gratefulness for what was right in front of her. When you start practicing gratitude therapy, living as a forgiver seems more natural because you are aware of how blessed, blessed, blessed you really are.

So, your journey begins today, my friend.

May I pray with you?

Thank You Father, for the heart of Your daughter that longs to live as a forgiver. Thank You for who she is. Thank You for this new life! Thank You in advance for walking with her through the tougher parts and for dancing in celebration with her as she climbs over those mountains to the other side.

Right now she may not fully understand where You are taking her, but she has signed up for the journey! She is courageous. She is expectant. Regardless of whether others change or not, she is holding her hands and heart up to You to receive transformation.

I raise my hands with her and thank You for all that You have already done. And I thank You for all that is to be performed with the power of the Holy Spirit, covered by Your grace, and bathed in Your purpose for each of us. In Your loving, mighty name, amen.

Suzie

Q & A

Earlier, I told you that six courageous woman worked with me as I wrote *The Unburdened Heart*. They were all ages, with differing stories and in various stages of healing, ranging from "Don't want to do this, but I'll read your stupid book" to "I've been trying for a long time, and I want something more." As they asked most of their questions, we delved deeper into Scripture, and that showed up in the chapters.

These are some of the questions that emerged as they were in the trenches of living out forgiveness afterwards.

Perhaps you are asking similar questions today.

Q: *Why do I need God to do something for me if He has already equipped me with the tools to do it myself?*

A: Because you may not know how to use the tools yet. In Romans 8:26-27, Paul says that the Holy Spirit helps us in our weakness. As we read this passage, we find that not only may we not know how to use the tools, but we also might not even know how to find the tools or what to do with them when we do locate them. According to this teaching, the Holy Spirit prays for you according to God's best for your life, then He leads you to the place that needs work, with the right tools at your disposal, and He gives you the wisdom to use those tools in the right way.

Q: *How am I supposed to feel about people when I've forgiven them? I have trouble feeling any kind of warm, loving feelings for them. Does that mean I haven't truly forgiven?*

A: Oh, those pesky feelings. They do get in the way, don't they?

God made us emotional beings. My friend and Proverbs 31 Ministries ministry team partner, Lysa TerKeurst, calls this wrestling match with emotions an "invitation to imperfect progress." She says in her book *Unglued:*

Sometimes we girls think if we don't make instant progress, then real change isn't coming. But that's not so.
There is a beautiful reality called imperfect progress. The
day I realized the glorious hope of this kind of imperfect
change is the day I gave myself permission to believe I
really could be different.[1]

You don't know how to feel in the beginning, and that's understandable. Don't force it. Let God do the work. Emotions such as
shame, sadness and pain lessen as we forgive. Celebrate each small
step toward healing. Mark the day that laughter overtakes sadness.
Praise God when compassion pushes over into the territory once
marked anger. It's imperfect progress, but it's progress, and it's
God's work inside of you as you intentionally pursue Him and all
that He has offered you as a forgiver.

Q: *I want to be strong enough to show those people that their indifference
or neglect won't stop me or slow me down, and that I don't need them. I
have convinced myself that it's safer to stay strong, stubborn and aloof.*

A: It's funny that what we call *strength* is often a defense mechanism. In the introduction, I shared how I had learned some unhealthy lessons. One of them was "I don't need anyone; I can do it
myself." This could be labeled self-sufficiency or independence,
but when I was finally able to be brutally honest, I called it what it
was. It was unforgiveness, and it had a purpose. It was a wall that
kept me in and people I thought might hurt me out. Dr. Charles
F. Stanley, in his book *The Gift of Forgiveness*, describes stages of an
unforgiving spirit. Here is one:

We try to schedule around our heart, that is, to arrange
our thought patterns and life in general so that we never
come into contact with anything that reminds us of our
hurt (an undertaking that is rarely successful), [and] we
attempt to forget the whole thing ever occurred. We dig a
hole and bury it as deeply as we can.[2]

This act serves like a foxhole in combat. We hunker down to avoid enemy fire, but the problem is that we are still stuck in the foxhole years after the initial battle has ended. Sometimes we drag our friends and family into that hole with us and they get wounded by friendly fire. You might be saying, "I don't need you" or "I don't want to be hurt"; but what happens when you begin to say, "I need You, God" and "Even if it opens me to additional hurt, I'm no longer trapped behind these walls. I'm free to discover who I was meant to be"?

The words *I need you* are first spoken to God, then to those closest to you. Eventually, as you heal, the words are spoken to those who may or may not receive them. Not all of them will receive it, but you become strong enough to voice them. Regardless of the response, you acknowledge that you are a woman who needs people and needs to live life open to love. You don't walk around wounded anymore; and if someone still is, you don't embrace his or her brokenness. You see it for what it is, and compassion and wisdom tell you how to feel, instead of the mess or chaos.

Q: I am afraid that a second and third chance will mean nothing. It will never bring about change.

A: Let's look at this two ways. First, we have to sort through what forgiveness is and what it's not. If an addict asks elderly grandparents for money, lies to them and uses it for drugs, there is an offense. The grandparents can freely forgive the grandchild for the lie, for stealing from them and for using their relationship and love to manipulate them for his or her own means. But this is where the grandparents might become confused about forgiving. If they say, "If we forgive, we'll trust them next time, and the next, no matter how many times they hurt us or lie to us," then the grandchild, in most cases, continues on in his or her destructive sin and the consequences.

However, if they say, "We see that addiction is a bully, and it's taking you down a path that God never intended. We will pray for you. We will never stop loving you. We will always believe that God can and will heal you, and that there is more for you," then that's a heart open to love, and it is forgiving over and over again.

Perhaps 7 times. Perhaps 49 times. Perhaps 490 times.

This heart to forgive is offered as they stop shielding their beautiful, much-loved-by-God grandchild from the consequences of addiction, lying and sin. Forgiving is an action and attitude of the heart. The action is always one of mercy, but mercy isn't defined by helping a person remain bound to sin as you bear the consequences and they never have to face that sin.

Second, you're afraid the person might not change if you forgive him or her. Let's just put it out there. He or she might not! You want them to. You hope they do. But none of us can climb into the heart of another person and bring about change. There are things you can do. You can show her love and show her Jesus. One of the most powerful ways to bring about change is for her to see Jesus' peace and joy inside of you, in spite of her choices. You are trusting God as your Source and to be the Source for your loved one.

Q: How do I let go of the need to guard myself against all other hurts if the change only occurs in me?

A: Let's imagine a wall. It's thick concrete. It is high. It's like a safe room. Nothing can get in. Nothing can get out. But do you want to live behind a wall every day for the rest of your life? I don't. My guess is that you don't either.

I was ministering in Arkansas to a small group of women. I described that wall of safety and how it's safe in there but also lonely. I admitted that when you ask God to take down that wall you might feel vulnerable. After all, there are a lot of people walking around who might say something or do something offensive or hurtful.

One woman admitted that very few people really knew her. Her wall was a very polite wall that kept people at a distance.

"What's behind that wall?" I asked.

"A fun person. I love music. I love to be silly," she said with a smile, "but I would never let that part of me out. It's just too risky."

Her wall was built by childhood abuse, by a man who was sent to prison for hurting her, and by people who judged her for her choices. She was a believer and loved God, but that wall even kept her from doing anything in the church for fear that she might mess up and be hurt.

I told her that our walls present a choice. Do we want to be 100 percent completely safe, but isolated and lonely? Or do we want to fly free? Let's just put it on the table. People are a work in progress. They might say something hurtful or unkind. They might not get your personality. (Sometimes we do the same and we don't even know it.)

But perfection is not our focus. What people, who struggle with their own issues, say or do isn't our focus. Our focus is living free. So we invite God to come in with a sledgehammer and knock down that wall. He's our Safety. He's our Shelter. And when we are hurt, He's our Comfort. Our Shield. Our Banner. Our Mighty Fortress!

Breaking down the wall means that you walk in wisdom. You weigh your decisions, your actions and responses and your relationships in light of Scripture and the fruit of the Spirit (see Gal. 5:22-23). You do these things with tools like gentleness, self-control, kindness, faithfulness and goodness.

You live free, but you don't live without encountering difficult people or challenges. However, you meet people and challenges hand in hand with your heavenly Father.

That day, my new friend walked out the door. As she held it open, she laughed and said, "I feel the wind. My walls are down. I'm going to fly."

Q: *The ultimate risk for me is the truth I'll need to face about myself and the hurt I've caused others. How do I face that and still have hope?*

A: I once overheard someone talking about a friend who was so stuck. She said, "She doesn't even know what she doesn't know." The last thing any of us really wants is to walk around clueless. We feel stuck. We want more. We feel that God has more. But that often takes place in those light-bulb moments when the Holy Spirit gently reveals an area where God wants to work.

Not too long ago, I saw a negative behavior in someone that I also recognized in myself. Ouch! I knew how it felt when it was directed at me, and as I drove home, the Lord showed me a couple of instances where I had done the same thing.

Choice point!

I could make an excuse. I could ignore it. I could get offended at God. Or I could accept with joy that my heavenly Father loves me enough to show me areas that keep me bound, so that I can grow. The next time I had the opportunity to exhibit that negative behavior, I held back. Up until that time, I had always thought it was just silly fun (teasing); but the Lord showed me the heart behind it, and it wasn't pretty.

Do I still tease? Sure. It's my nature to be playful with loved ones, but I also won't ignore that there is something (Someone) inside of me that makes me pause to check my heart and motivation.

Listen, there's power in the apology. You will make mistakes. But the truth, and all that God is showing you today, is so that you can grow in your faith and in your relationship with Him and with others. That's a powerful gift. Throw guilt out and look forward to what God is doing inside of you!

Notes

1. Lysa TerKeurst, *Unglued: Making Wise Choices in the Midst of Raw Emotions* (Grand Rapids, MI: Zondervan, 2012), p. 14.

2. Charles Stanley, *The Gift of Forgiveness* (Nashville, TN: Thomas Nelson, 1991).

About Suzanne Eller

Suzie (as friends call her) is passionate to come alongside women and lead them in a new direction in the areas of family, feelings and faith. Suzie is an author and an international speaker with Proverbs 31 Ministries. She is also a radio co-host on the syndicated radio show Encouragement Café with Luann and friends (www.encouragementcafe.com).

She is a cancer survivor and loves life to the fullest.

She is a mom, wife and Gramma who lives in beautiful green country—Oklahoma. When Suzie is not writing or speaking, you'll find her hiking, running 5Ks, in her garden or rafting down a river. If you are interested in having Suzie be a keynote speaker or speak at your church or women's conference on this or other topics, please contact Proverbs 31 Ministries.

If you were inspired by *The Unburdened Heart,* and you desire to deepen your own personal relationship with Jesus Christ, I encourage you to connect with Proverbs 31 Ministries.

Proverbs 31 Ministries exists to be a trusted friend that will take you by the hand and walk by your side, leading you one step closer to the heart of God through these resources:

- *Encouragement for Today*, online daily devotions
- The *P31 Woman* monthly magazine
- Daily radio program
- Books and resources

- Dynamic speakers with life-changing messages
- Online Bible studies
- Gather and Grow Groups and online communities

To learn more about Proverbs 31 Ministries, or to inquire about having Suzanne Eller speak at your event, call 877-731-4663 or visit www.proverbs31.org.

Proverbs 31 Ministries
630 Team Road, Suite 100
Matthews, NC 28105
www.Proverbs31.org